'How 'Bout Them Claymores!'

ABOUT THE AUTHORS

MIKE DAVIDSON is a veteran sports journalist, reporter, columnist and respected editor who has followed and covered American football since the 1970s. A former sports editor with *The Daily Record*, Mike now reports on the World League and National Football League for *The Scottish Daily Mail*. Also a keen follower of baseball, Mike's favourite NFL team is the Miami Dolphins.

STEVE LIVINGSTONE, a freelance journalist and former amateur gridiron player with the Glasgow Diamonds, Edinburgh Eagles and Glasgow Lions, covers the World League and NFL for *The Herald*. When not writing about the sport he continues to remain active in gridiron as an amateur college head football coach with his alma mater, University of Strathclyde Hawks.

ANDY COLVIN is *The Scottish Sun*'s American football writer. One of the premier gridiron writers in Britain, Andy has covered the World League and NFL for the last ten years. Committed to excellence as a hardened Oakland Raiders fanatic, Colvin's in-depth Claymores player features during the past two World League seasons have earned him plaudits not only from the critics, but also from the players themselves.

RODDY McKENZIE covers a myriad of sports as a correspondent with the Edinburgh Sports Reporting Service, supplying stories for many of Scotland's top newspapers. A keen follower of American football, McKenzie has covered the NFL since the 1980s and the Claymores since their inception.

GORDON SCOTT is a sports reporter with *The Edinburgh Evening News* and a recent convert to the American game. Known for his in-depth feature stories, Scott's many Claymores articles have been instrumental in 'taking the helmet off the player' and turning Claymores stars into household names.

WAYNE PAULO is a respected freelance photographer with an eye for gridiron. As the Claymores' team photographer for the past two seasons, Paulo has captured the many varied moments behind the Claymores' remarkable story.

Edited by WIL WILSON

Special thanks to DAWN PETERSON for her help and article on the cheerleaders, and to STEVE LIVINGSTONE for his hard work and suggestions.

THE MURRAYFIELD MIRACLE

'How 'bout them CLAYMORES!'

MAINSTREAM
PUBLISHING

EDINBURGH AND LONDON

First published in Great Britain in 1996 by
MAINSTREAM PUBLISHING COMPANY
(EDINBURGH) LTD
7 Albany Street
Edinburgh EH1 3UG

ISBN 1 85158 925 2

Typeset in Times
Designed by Janene Reid
Printed and bound in Great Britain by
Butler & Tanner Ltd, Frome

CONTENTS

FOREWORD

When the Scottish Claymores first initiated the idea of me playing for their World League team I was admittedly sceptical. But as a sportsman I was secretly intrigued. I knew that the Claymores were a first-class organisation through my own business association with them. But could 20 years of kicking a ball rugby style be transferred to the techniques required for the professional American game?

In the end my curiosity and love of a new challenge won out, and after a trial session at the Denver Broncos in America, I decided I would give it a go and join the team for training camp in Georgia. Needless to say, I am extremely happy that I made that decision.

And what a season it was. From my first successful kick against the London Monarchs in the first week of the season to our World Bowl victory in front of 40,000 fans at Murray-field, I was introduced into the life of a professional American footballer and developed an appreciation for the game which I'm sure I will never lose.

Enjoy the following highlights of our championship-winning season.

GAVIN HASTINGS

INTRODUCTION

'How 'Bout Them Claymores!' is a story about the success of a team. When most people think of a team, they imagine a group of athletes who perform in front of cheering fans. The Claymores' successful 1996 season, culminating with victory in the World Bowl, was so much more. It is a story of many groups of people who contributed behind the scenes as well as on the field. It is about the 12 months of dedicated work that led to a championship held at Murrayfield on 23 June 1996 in front of nearly 40,000 sunbathed, ecstatic followers. Most of all, it is a story of the introduction of a sport into a hopeful but sceptical nation of sports enthusiasts and the distance that that sport has come in such a short period of time.

Rising out of the ashes of a disastrous 1995 season, Jim Criner began assembling a group of coaches who would begin the painstaking process of self-evaluation that would lead to the miracle at Murrayfield on 23 June. In similar fashion the administration of the Claymores would begin its own rebuilding process that would, at the end, share the accolades of the football operation.

A rebuilding process in any endeavour is nearly always more difficult than building from scratch. In a rebuilding process a team has to undo and overcome before it sets itself on a path towards success. The high hopes and interest the Claymores generated initially in 1995 were given a sobering dose of reality when the season spiralled downward to a league-worst two-win, eight-loss season.

It would take more than hard work to turn it around; it would take equal doses of creativity, imagination, showmanship, skill and luck. Fortunately, the Claymores' team had all of these virtues in abundance. Jim Criner and his coaches were building bridges with our National Football League counterparts in the United States. They were putting the pieces of a championship puzzle together. In Scotland the new Claymores were creating an image of professionalism as well as a reputation as an aggressive and innovative marketing organisation. Marketing director John Hall, assisted by Norman Sutherland, Paul Blanchard and Gavin Hastings, listened to sponsors and developed creative packages that began to gather attention. The Kwik-Fit fitters and their D-Fence routine and Wimpy Homes Kids Area are solid examples. McCann-Erickson and their staff of advertising pros led by Aubrey Malden began setting the stage to translate growing respect into avid followers. Alan Smith led the effort to establish the Claymores' shop on George Street and suddenly people in Scotland could see the Claymores were serious about establishing themselves and laying the groundwork for future success.

Attempts made to convince people that the new Claymores meant business and to turn the entire 1995 disappointment around were being met with ample amounts of scepticism. Equally apparent was the 'who do you think you are?' attitude for bringing a foreign sport to a land that was doing just fine without it. New ways of promoting the Claymores and gridiron football were needed.

We decided that value and convenience with ample doses of professionalism were needed. Lowered ticket prices, open seating and better entertainment on the Murrayfield backfields got the ball rolling. Recognising that Claymores games offered a safe, family environment coupled with first-class entertainment was the final ingredient that set the stage for the season. Now all that was needed was a win or two.

Criner was wearing out his eyes looking at film, and his assistants, led by Ray Willsey, Jim Sochor and Scottish national coach Michael Kenny, were putting their player list together. A catalyst was needed and that catalyst was spelled Siran Stacy. Stacy was a shining star for the '95 Claymores in a dark and dismal season. Leading the league in

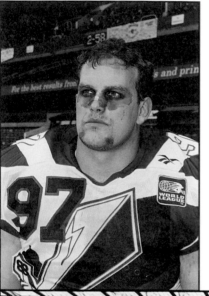

rushing on the worst World League team was a monumental accomplishment. A target of every World League tackler, Siran never quit. He inspired his team-mates to finish '95 on a positive note in the Claymores' final game of the season, a win over the Monarchs in London.

A great season and a determined effort failed to move an NFL team to sign him for an opportunity in the US-based league. Disappointed, Stacy was leaning towards retiring from the World League and returning to school. Numerous calls between Criner, myself, Stacy and Stacy's mentor, Gene Stallings of Alabama, led to Stacy's decision to give it one more try, and what a try it's been. On the ground or through the air, Stacy was an unstoppable force in the Claymores' drive to the title. Joining forces with a stellar offensive line, great quarterbacking and a receiving corps led by Sean LaChapelle, Yo Murphy and Scott Couper, it looked like points wouldn't be a problem for the Claymores.

The coaching staff drafted Ty Parten on to the team to join

returning stalwarts Mark Sander, George Coghill and Jerold Jeffcoat, and a rock-solid defensive group was taking shape.

It was obvious to me that we had the makings of a team to be reckoned with. We had the ingredients; now we needed some fire to temper them into a solid unit. That came immediately in our opening game in London. The Claymores trailed by 14 points at half-time and even this early it appeared the season hung in the balance. The team clawed back to tie the game with a Gavin Hastings conversion – as pressure-packed as any he would ever kick. The Claymores never looked back and fought their way through the ups and downs of an 11-week season. Through injuries and losses the focus was never lost.

Standing on the podium receiving the World Bowl trophy, we experienced the euphoria of knowing that we had just capped a memorable turnaround from worst to first. Seeing 40,000 spectators celebrate by singing *Flower of Scotland* was a feeling to cherish. All who were there, Scots and non-Scots alike, will look back on the memory with fond thoughts.

Let me also mention maybe the most important member of our team: 'The Twelfth Man'. It is the tradition in the US that gridiron teams refer to the fans who help their team win as the twelfth man on the squad. We couldn't have achieved our goals, nor would the

championship have been as sweet, without the outpouring of support we received from the best fans in the World League. Through good weather and bad you came out to participate in our growing story. Especially the children, the youngsters with the painted faces dragging mum and dad around the backfield and into the stadium. They are the future of our sport and the future is bright.

Commissioner Tagliabue, Neil Austrian and Roger Goodell of the National Football League offered solid advice and unflagging support for our efforts, all the while believing that success would come. They joined with the owners, coaches, management and players of the NFL to see the benefits of bringing gridiron football to Europe and had the foresight to allow it to grow in largely uninterested markets.

The NFL was joined by Fox Sports and George Kreiger in showing the visible spectacle that is the World League to millions of viewers. The quality of World League telecasts adds to the growing respect for the World League. Growth is assured when quality entertainment is shown professionally and sold with enthusiasm.

Finally, let me mention that the success of any operation such as the Claymores succeeds largely as a result of the hard work of those who often toil in anonymity. Wil Wilson and Dawn Peterson communicated with the media and promoted the Claymores throughout Scotland. Steve Wilde and his Day of Game staff put on the best party and most organised stadium operation in the World League. Nancy Cressey, Alison Lawrie, Anna Clark and Nicola Will supported hospitality and put casual, relaxed hospitality on the map and smiles on the faces of all who attended.

Enjoy this story about a rags-to-riches group of people who came together to do something right. 'How 'Bout Them Claymores!'

MICHAEL F. KELLER
General Manager

Whatever doubts that may have been harboured about the validity of the World League of American Football – a bold gamble by the NFL and Fox TV to establish a gridiron niche in the psyche of European professional sports – were swept aside one sunlit June evening in 1996 in the magnificent setting of Murrayfield Stadium. That night the Scottish Claymores completed their metamorphosis from the dull-edged nightmare of their debut season in '95 to become World Bowl champions and, in doing so, presented Scotland – and the league – with a unique global triumph.

The thrilling 32–27 victory over the Frankfurt Galaxy on 23 June 1996 was the culmination of a roller-coaster ride from worst to first, witnessed by a near-40,000 crowd in Murrayfield and an international TV audience estimated at 200 million, all of whom were mesmerised by the sheer magnetism of the event. And it proved to the sceptics what WLAF president Oliver Luck had been so sure of all along – that this second incarnation of the league, after a two-year hiatus in '93–94, was here for good and that expansion was the next

logical step. The Claymores had demonstrated that the fusion of NFL-calibre players with a significant national contribution, sound coaching, shrewd marketing and a true sense of identity were the not-so-secret secrets of success.

The green light for establishing high-class, international professional American football was signalled in 1988, when the NFL owners (then 28 but now 30) endorsed a feasibility study which called for a ten-team, three-division league comprising London, Barcelona and Frankfurt in Europe, New York-New Jersey, Montreal, Orlando and Raleigh-Durham in the North American East Division and Birmingham, San Antonio and Sacramento in the west.

Armed with TV deals with ABC, USA Cable, Channel 4 and other local networks, the league kicked off on 23 March 1991, and on 9 June that year the London Monarchs crowned the inaugural season by winning the first ever World Bowl, beating the Barcelona Dragons 20–0 at Wembley before a sell-out crowd of 61,108 – still the biggest audience at any World League

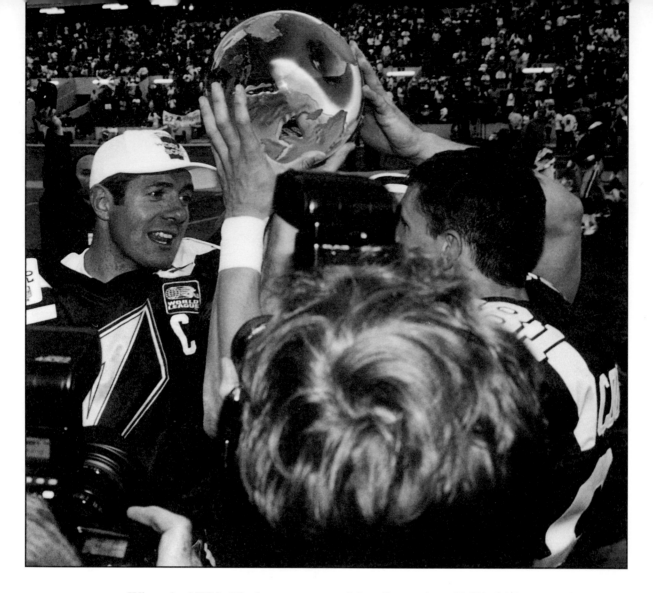

game. When the NFL's 72nd season opened that September, 29 World Leaguers had made it onto the rosters.

The Ohio Glory replaced Raleigh-Durham for the '92 season, but it was the Sacramento Surge who emerged as champions after a 21–17 victory over the Orlando Thunder in Montreal. National Football League training camps opened with 219 of the 360 World Leaguers signed to contracts, so the practicality of the operation as a grooming ground for full NFL participation was undeniable. The glittering example is Scott Mitchell, who had quarterbacked Orlando. After going on to back up the legendary Dan Marino at Miami, he signed a fabulous $11 million, three-year deal with the Detroit Lions.

However, fans in the States, as ever beguiled and sated by the magic of the NFL, were slow to respond to the WLAF in some areas and that contributed to the decision to suspend and restructure. Thus was conceived in 1995 the six-club all-European alliance, a $40 million, four-year joint venture between the NFL and Fox, with Sky carrying the action live in Britain and highlights shown on Scottish Television and Channel 4. The Claymores, the

Amsterdam Admirals and the Rhein Fire were created to join the three original Euro franchises, each club playing ten times in the regular season, home and away, for the right to contest the World Bowl.

The Claymores represented the league's biggest risk, introduced into a country with none of the long-established American traditions in place in Germany, or a base of pre-season NFL show-games that Wembley could boast. So, label it how you will – from outhouse to penthouse, rags to riches, to hell and back – the Claymores' story reads like the script for the movie blockbuster *Reversal of Fortune* (which just happened to be an Oscar-winner). It seems the plundering of World Bowl was the preordained reward for an incredible chapter in American football's book of lore.

A team born in hope, then scarred by controversy, survived a soul-destroying first year of existence to emerge, 12 months later, as the dominant force. It's not supposed to happen that way in a sport that needs the crucial element of time to forge true champions. But the WLAF is a hurry-up league dealing in quick-fire miracles.

The sum of many parts makes up the Claymores' whole, so it would be entirely unfair to single out any one man from the 50 or so who became part of the sporting story of the decade. In 1996 Siran Stacy smashed World League records for rushing and all-purpose yards from scrimmage, Sean LaChapelle became the season's most feared receiver, Jim Ballard produced incredible pass-completion and scoring statistics when he replaced injured starter Steve Matthews to quarterback the team in the last three and a half games. And when LaChapelle went down with a first-half groin injury in the World Bowl, Yo Murphy stepped from his shadow to snag three blistering touchdown catches and the game's Most Valuable Player award.

Every single member of the defence made a huge contribution to the winning of the first half of the season, the vital ingredient in ensuring that the World Bowl would be staged at Murrayfield. And they were a key factor as the Claymores compiled a 7–3 record, best in the league. But if someone was to demand a point in time when the first hint surfaced that the Claymores might grasp their destiny by the scruff of the neck and become the flashing blades of history, it might have to be the moment when Gavin Hastings decided to put the boot in.

Hindsight is a wonderful resource for seeing clearly now what might have been slightly obscure way back then, but the Claymores could not have targeted a more qualified athlete than Hastings to be their lightning rod. Here was no burnt-out soccer player, no spent force of track and field looking for an easy pay-day. At 34, Hastings had done it all on the rugby field. A record 544 points, most conversions (68) and most penalty goals (121) in the book for Scotland, a Grand Slam, Lions tours, a wonderful World Cup and a record-setting 61 Scotland caps – a feat only bettered by brother Scott – had merely sated his international appetite.

Club rugby with Watsonians and the expansion of Hastings International, his marketing consultancy – part of whose clientele just happen to be the Claymores – were to be his '96 priorities . . . until the siren call of one last hurrah, the chance to kick again in the blue of Scotland, proved too tempting to resist. The first seeds were sown during a covert kicking session in the rarified atmosphere of the Denver Broncos' training facility in December. 'I broke off a skiing holiday to do that,' Hastings reveals. 'And I didn't miss a kick there, so obviously it concentrated my thoughts on the idea of trying out for the Claymores.'

A growing personal and professional relationship with new general manager Mike Keller excited more serious consideration – then followed an inspirational and persuasive day in the company of NFL commissioner Paul Tagliabue. 'I'm a positive guy and they both laid out a very positive case for joining the Claymores. They definitely helped me make up my mind,' Hastings admits. 'I had to make some tough decisions to come to that point. About whether I had a genuine chance to do the job properly. Whether what I was about to do might compromise my rugby. But people who know me realise I'm not one to shirk a challenge when I resolve to take it on.

'I did not for a minute think it was going to be easy. I'm not exactly stupid, and I knew that kicking casually on my own was like day and night compared to the stress of doing it surrounded by rather large opponents full of bad intentions. But I would have hated to reject the idea before giving it a real go. That type of thinking can leave you regretting for years what might have been. You never know until you try.'

So the die was cast and Hastings would go to training camp in Carrollton, near Atlanta, in March to subject himself to the severest of personal examinations and take a crash course in a game he knew little about, laying his reputation on the line before players and coaches whose grasp of and familiarity with every nuance of the sport was virtually inbred after generations of refinement.

'He will be an invaluable asset in our championship season,' was how Keller prophetically put it. Hastings added realistically: 'Whether I make it or not, I will have given it my best shot' – knowing full well that his giant reputation on the rugby field would mean nothing once he donned the helmet and body-armour of the gridiron. It took guts for Scotland's highest-profile sportsman to fly in the face of so many gainsayers – those closed minds, brainwashed by the sacrosanct concept of soccer and rugby, who reacted to innovation with an ostrich-like penchant for head-in-the-sand antipathy. Eventually even they, grudgingly, had to shake off the grains of scepticism as the rest of the story, along with Hastings, blossomed into a glowing chapter in the annals of professional football.

To appreciate fully the total transformation wrought by head coach Jim Criner and his hand-picked assistants, you must make the painful journey back in time to the grey, overcast spring of 1995, when the Claymores' birth-pangs were dampened by raindrops of dissension and chilled by a bitter April wind of change.

First-choice supremo Lary Kuharich had been fired five days before the Claymores' inaugural game. His heavy-handed, brutally divisive man-management sparked unprecedented alarm during training camp in Atlanta, lighting the smouldering touchpaper of resentment which flamed into full-blown rebellion on the backfields of Murrayfield. Criner, offensive co-ordinator and a successful college coach of long standing, was handed his first professional head coaching job in circumstances he could never have foreseen. Kuharich was gone and so was his playbook – the gridiron bible which holds the keys to executing the gameplan. It was pick-up-the-pieces time.

Ten weeks later, Criner had managed to wring just two wins from the schedule, in Frankfurt, against the eventual World Bowl 95 champions, and in London in the season's final game. But nothing at home to warm the Murrayfield faithful. And yet . . . And yet . . . The Claymores had been embarrassed three times – manhandled twice by Amsterdam and once by Frankfurt in the final home game of that year – but the five other losses, four by three points or less and the other in overtime, could so easily have been victories.

Criner knew he had the nucleus of a good side. 'It was damned hard trying to explain away these narrow defeats,' he says. 'Especially to some of the fans who were new to the game. But we had the makings of a fine defence and running back Siran Stacy, with more consistent support, was a potent offensive weapon. I was sure, if I could get the coaches I wanted and the returning players I needed, we could build something. We did just that, and then we had an outstanding draft.'

Criner, indeed, extracted almost everything he desired, including go-getter Keller – a man with that penetrating look of eagles that leaves you in no doubt about his utter disdain for failure – brought in to streamline the administrative and marketing departments. With his reputation as a franchise-builder already made in the now-defunct United States Football League, Keller was the front office barn-burner with Sacramento in their World Bowl triumph of 1992, when Criner was the offensive co-ordinator. And Mike played clean-up for '95 World Bowl winners Frankfurt, where Ray Willsey was defensive co-ordinator and now Criner's inspired choice for the same role with the Claymores.

A long-time friendship with Criner tempted college record-breaker Jim Sochor into taking a sabbatical from the University of Cal-Davis to produce his variations on the enduring West Coast system as offensive co-ordinator. Larry Owens arrived to influence the linebackers and Vince Alcalde came in to oversee the receivers. Bill Dutton, defensive line guru *par excellence*, was a holdover from '95, as was national coach Mike Kenny, to fine-tune the running backs.

The NFL allocation draft was a dazzler. Criner's Kansas City connection attracted Sean LaChapelle, pass-blocking guard Tom Barndt, emerging tight end Willy Tate, quarterback Steve Matthews, who started the first eight games of '96, and defensive tackle Bryan Proby, who overcame playing time restricted by injury to be a World Bowl stand-out. But the growing willingness by the NFL clubs to support the World League also brought super centre Lance Zeno from the LA Rams, giant guard Purvis Hunt (Houston Oilers), tackle Keith Wagner (Washington Redskins), guard Matt Storm (Washington Redskins), receiver Lee Gissendaner (Minnesota Vikings) and corner Forey Duckett (New Orleans).

The open draft itself was testimony to the coaches' painstaking, close-season assessments. Defensive tackle Ty Parten was the overall No. 1 pick and lived up to his status. Then there were Shannon Jones, Yo Murphy, John DeWitt, Frank Robinson, Arnold Ale, Ron Dickerson, Herman Carroll, Joe O'Brien, Jared Kaaiohelo and James Fuller, the last a last-minute, diamond-studded pick-up after his release by Frankfurt.

Then there were the guys who were in place for the Claymores' difficult birth – and came back for more. Men with a mission to explain why there had to be no reprise of '95's heartbreak. On defence the league's predominant safety George Coghill, ferocious middle linebacker Mark Sander and defensive end David Webb, nose guard Jerold Jeffcoat, cornerback James Williams, free safety David Wilson. On offence the incomparable Stacy, fellow rusher and special teamer Markus Thomas, tackle Randy Bierman, guard Matt Storm and blossoming Scots, receiver Scott Couper and gritty special-teams hitter Ben Torriero. All had a story to tell the newcomers – national recruit Gregor Maxwell from Aberdeen, Finnish recruit Jukka-Pekka Nummi, and Irish-born Houston University linebacker Emmett Waldron – about frustration and about depression, but above all they talked about self-belief.

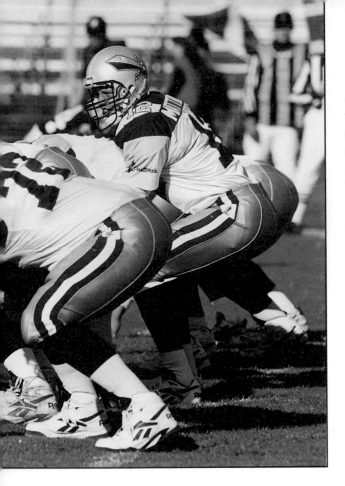

And, of course, there was Gav – the PR stroke of the decade, the Murrayfield legend who filled the seventh and last national spot and became a court jester in training camp. A true sporting superstar more than willing to become one of the guys again and the catalyst in bringing them together as a unit. Judge for yourselves who got the better deal when you compare the London Monarchs' circus signing of Monster Fridge William Perry, whose cheerful but lumbering contribution ended on injured reserve after eight weeks of the regular season.

Camp for World League of American footballers is the place of pain and sweat in which 60 hopefuls are punished pitilessly, then pruned perversely to produce an active roster of 41. Suited up for the first time in the Claymore colours, Hastings soon discovered the vast gulf in technique required to kick rugby penalties and conversions, as he so often and so productively did for Scotland, and convert a field goal or extra point on the gridiron.

However, aided by the man who would become the Claymores' field goal kicker, Scots-Canadian Paul McCallum, he gradually got used to the nuances needed for kick-offs – and the natural rhythm and timing required for the successful conversion of an extra point, which should take just 1.2 seconds from the snap of the ball to the precise grounding of it by the holder seven yards back in time for the swing of the Hastings right boot.

'I committed myself to camp to learn and hoped to come back a fully fledged kicker for the Claymores,' he says. 'And Paul was a terrific help to me, even though we were competing for the same job. He is a class act.' Passing his physical with flying colours, Hastings learned about the necessity of team-meetings, boned up on the rules and came to terms with play calls and gameplans. 'Then it was a question of practice,' Hastings says. 'Repetition after repetition until the whole routine became second nature. I thought I did pretty well for a new boy, but it was only towards the end of camp that things really clicked for me.'

It was then that kicking legend Morten Anderson and Mick Luckhurst, the NFL's most successful British-born kicker and one-time Channel 4 presenter, analysed the mechanics of Hastings's action. He had been using a cut-down version of his 'banana-shaped' rugby approach to the ball and they quickly persuaded him to forego it completely for a right-angled run-up. 'I had been doing things in a way I felt comfortable,' Hastings explains. 'But Morten and Mick straightened me out, and the adjustments they made improved my kicking dramatically.'

But the scrimmaging at Carrollton was no ego trip for the team. Competence against

London and a 47-yard field goal into the teeth of the wind to beat Frankfurt were memories Hastings could savour. But the Claymores' farewell to Atlanta was a good old-fashioned 35–10 thumping by Amsterdam. While admitting they had been soundly outplayed, head coach Criner said much later: 'Nobody liked getting turned over by these other guys. But maybe it set up some revenge to shoot for when the season began. We certainly kept a few things back for the real thing.'

So, still confident but now far from complacent, the Claymores headed home with most of the pieces in place for the end-game on the human chessboard that is the gridiron. There was, however, one more master move to be made, the importance of which cannot be

minimised. While keeping the front office, admin and sales in Edinburgh, the Claymores decanted the team west from Silverknowes on the outskirts of Edinburgh to stay in Glasgow's Central Hotel and train, in-season, at Strathclyde University's dedicated facility in Stepps.

Quickly, morale soared and team spirit solidified. Players welded together from six countries finally felt at home. 'The only thing that hasn't got better around here is the weather,' said one grizzled WLAF veteran in May. 'But who cares when you have a team feeling as good as this one.'

As the season's start approached, Hastings knew he would be used to kick off and to convert extra points, while McCallum would be taking punts and hitting field goals. 'I was still pretty pleased with my form at Stepps,' says Hastings. 'I even managed to kick a 50-yard field goal in practice, so the tips I got in Atlanta were bearing fruit.' He was to be put to the test immediately in the Claymores' opener in London against the Monarchs.

The triumphal march to World Bowl 96 glory is described vividly in subsequent pages and, obviously, the feeling of elation when the title was won will be a memory Hastings cherishes for ever, along with his team-mates. Assessing the pluses and minuses of his own contribution – 23 extra points scored from 27 attempted – he says frankly: 'I felt I was a better kicker in the first half of the season than I was at the end, but that may be down to the pressure. Pressure we all felt increasing as the big game got closer.

'In a rugby game you are constantly involved in the action. A kicker in American football spends most of his time on the sidelines watching and waiting for his moment. It takes a lot of getting used to and can be a severe test of your concentration. The point after touchdown may appear a small part of the game and look a simple thing to do, but I can assure you it is not. Your opponents make sure of that. And the slightest distraction can disrupt the essential rhythm between the kicker, the centre who snaps the ball back and the holder who spots it.

'The guys who kick for a living in the NFL have my utmost admiration. They do what they do in the full glare of the spotlight and the fans think they should never miss. Now I know what goes into landing a successful kick and I salute their nerve. Of course I would have loved to have had a mistake-free season, but few players ever do. I only attempted one field goal and missed it in the second time we played London. But I had waited eight and a half weeks for the chance and that induces its own kind of tension. Maybe I was a bit too tight. Anyway, it was a bit of a blow to fail but, all in all, I am happy that I did well and did not let the team down.'

Kicking the ball off to the opposition – to start the game or restart it after your team has scored – is an art in itself and Hastings feels he improved in that department as the season progressed. 'We scored a couple of touchdowns in the World Bowl from kick-offs that were mishandled by Frankfurt,' Hastings points out. 'When that happens you feel you've done your job properly.

'I feel privileged to have been a part of history,' says the only man to have experienced the thrill of winning a Grand Slam and a World Bowl. 'It's a shame the team which achieved so much have gone on to other things, but that's the way this league works. A lot will have moved on to the NFL, so you have to savour the moment while you can.'

THE SEASON IN REVIEW

Steve Livingstone and Andy Colvin

WEEK 1: HASTINGS'S SWEET CONVERSION

Scottish Claymores 24 at London Monarchs 21 (OT)

'We're going to be a much better football team this year than last,' promised Jim Criner as he put the finishing touches to the line-up that would kick off the 1996 World League season away to the heavily favoured London Monarchs, who featured newly signed NFL legend William 'The Refrigerator' Perry.

'Last season we were small and slow, this season we're big, strong and fast and we can't wait to get into the English,' added the coach. 'The key to winning will be for our defence to keep them off the board to allow our offence time to settle into their gameplan. We hope Sean LaChapelle, who has come from the Kansas City Chiefs, can put a lot of pressure on their defence.'

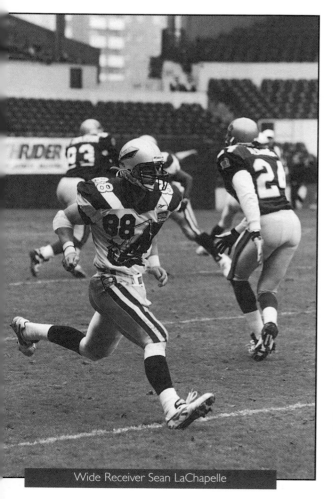

Wide Receiver Sean LaChapelle

That gameplan was in danger of being executed to perfection after safety James Fuller returned Sonny Feexico's opening kick-off 30 yards in front of the largely hostile 16,258 crowd at White Hart Lane. Three plays later, quarterback Steve Matthews floated an arching pass to wide receiver Yo Murphy, who made a stunning fingertip catch in the corner of the endzone for the Scots' first touchdown of the season. Gavin Hastings, as expected, didn't flinch on his debut, confidently booting through the extra point to get the Claymores off to a flying start.

But Criner's strategy was torn into shreds when Kenny McEntyre intercepted Matthews allowing London passer Preston Jones to link up with Atlanta Falcons allocated running back Tony Vinson on a ten-yard touchdown pass at the start of the second quarter. Kevin Hurst's PAT (point after touchdown) put the Monarchs level but the Londoners broke away on their next two possessions as the Claymores faltered.

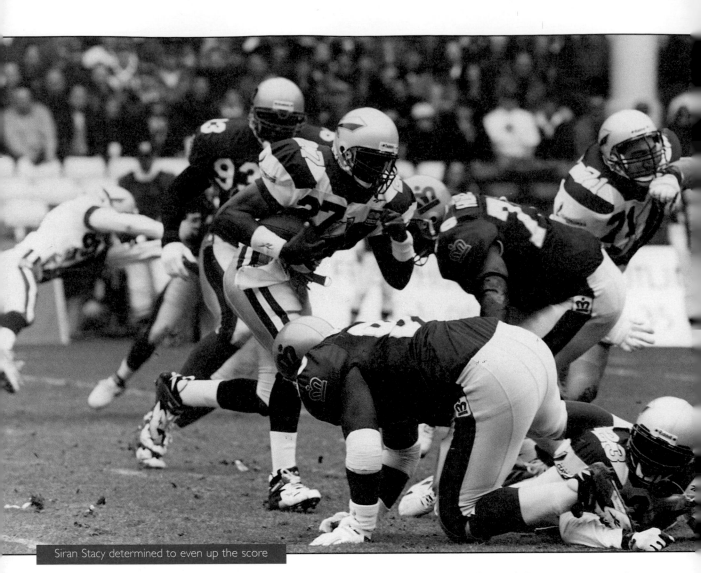

Siran Stacy determined to even up the score

First Jones connected with Gaston Green on a two-yard touchdown pass to take advantage of a Ron Dickerson fumble. Then the Monarchs posted a 21–7 half-time lead when Matthews threw up a second disastrous interception which was returned 21 yards for a touchdown by Monarchs' speedy cornerback Darren Studstill.

During the break Criner rallied his troops in the locker room and the Bravehearts came out fighting. Matthews hit LaChapelle with a 17-yard pass and two plays later running back Siran Stacy powered in on a one-yard score. Hastings's PAT brought the Scots to within a touchdown at 21–14. With 1:53 left in the game Matthews launched a 25-yard pass to LaChapelle, who showed tremendous concentration to catch the ball in the corner of the endzone, bringing the score to 21–20. Hastings, tested at the highest level during his international rugby career, coolly slotted through the extra point to tie the match. London kicker David Gordon then had a chance to win it for the Monarchs but pushed his 39-yard kick wide right, sending the game into overtime.

The Monarchs couldn't move it on their first extra-time possession and were forced to punt. The Claymores got back into scoring range when LaChapelle broke free on a 31-yard reception from Matthews. But Stacy was stuffed trying to run the ball in for the win and, after Dunstan Anderson sacked Matthews, Criner sent on-field goal kicker and punter, Paul McCallum, to win the game. McCallum, a Canadian Football League star, showed his nerves were as steely as Hastings's and slammed through the 27-yard field goal to give the Scots a remarkable come-from-behind victory, securing them the Budweiser Cup and a great start to their 1996 campaign.

Afterwards, Hastings said: 'I was more nervous than on any kick in my life – if I'd missed it, we'd have lost the game. What a confidence boost to me, and to the whole team, when it went over and Paul [McCallum] then kicked the winning field goal.' LaChapelle, who notched up 150 yards on seven receptions and one touchdown on his Claymores debut, said: 'I just happened to be in the right place at the right time. Steve Matthews deserves all the credit for putting the ball on the money for me.'

GAME STATISTICS

WEEK 1: SCOTTISH CLAYMORES at LONDON MONARCHS;
WHITE HART LANE, LONDON; 14 APRIL 1996; ATT: 16,258;
WEATHER: FAIR, 12°C

SCORE BY PERIODS

	1	2	3	4	OT	
CLAYMORES	7	0	7	7	3	24
MONARCHS	7	14	0	0	0	21

SCORING SUMMARY

Team	Period	Elapsed Time	Play	Score
Sco	1st	4:27	TD, Murphy 11 pass Matthews (Hastings PAT)	7-0
Lon	2nd	4:02	TD, Vinson 10 pass Jones (Hurst PAT)	7-7
Lon	2nd	13:43	TD, Green 2 pass Jones (Hurst PAT)	7-14
Lon	2nd	14:10	TD, Studstill 21 interception return (Hurst PAT)	7-21
Sco	3rd	7:48	TD, Stacy 1 run (Hastings PAT)	14-21
Sco	4th	13:07	TD, LaChapelle 25 pass Matthews (Hastings PAT)	21-21
Sco	OT	6:12	FG, McCallum 27	24-21

TEAM STATISTICS

	CLAYMORES	MONARCHS
First Downs	20	15
Rushes/Yards	23/71	25/77
Net Passing Yards	257	153
Total Net Yards	328	230
Passing (A-C-I)	43/21/4	36/18/1
Punts/Average	4/28.0	7/41.0
Fumbles/Lost	2/1	1/1
Penalties	4/35	6/55
Time of Possession	34:28	31:44

INDIVIDUAL STATISTICS

RUSHING

Claymores: Stacy 15-27-1; Matthews 4-26; Dickerson 4-18
Monarchs: White 12-33; Green 8-30; Jones 1-8; Vinson 4-6

PASSING

Claymores: Matthews 42-21-273, 2TD, 4INT; Karg 1-0, 0TD, 0INT
Monarchs: Jones 36-18-154, 2TD, 1INT

RECEIVING

Claymores: LaChapelle 7-150-1; Stacy 6-52; Murphy 3-32-1; Couper 2-15; Dickerson 5-15; Tate 1-9
Monarchs: Wallace 6-64; White 4-37; Green 3-6-1; Howard 2-17; Vinson 2-20-1; Hinchcliff 1-10

SEAN LaCHAPELLE: THE RELUCTANT RECEIVER

Ask Sean LaChapelle what he hates most about being a football player and he'll tell you straight: the limelight. Unfortunately for LaChapelle, his prodigious talent as a wide receiver ensures that he'll be saddled with the spotlight whether he likes it or not.

Allocated to the Claymores at his own request by the Kansas City Chiefs, LaChapelle rewrote the record books during the '96 season. He clocked up 1,023 receiving yards to eclipse the old record of 1,011 yards by Sacramento Surge star Eddie Brown back in 1992. That feat saw him voted Offensive Player of the Year by the World League's head coaches.

But his discomfort at attracting a high-profile image could just as easily have seen LaChapelle lost to football for good. Ranked sixth in the US for receptions after a stunning college career at UCLA, the Sacramento-born 26-year-old seemed destined for a glittering NFL career. Instead, disillusionment with the inflated egos within the NFL saw him quit the LA Rams in 1994 and consider packing in football altogether.

'I made a decision and I stand by it,' he said. 'I was burnt out. When I went to the Rams I wasn't prepared for how cut-throat professional football is. I couldn't cope with the egos of other NFL players. It soured my taste even more and it finally got to the stage where I didn't want to play football again.'

That LaChapelle eventually came back into football with the Chiefs is a testament to his love of the game. And nobody was happier that he took that decision than the Claymores fans as he pouched catch after catch to pull victories out of the fire last season. But the wide receiver insists he never gets caught up in the hype which is inevitably generated by his performances.

'It's great to do a job and that's all I care about,' he said. 'My concern is running the proper pass route and catching the ball if it comes my way. The day after I've hopefully done that job, well, it's yesterday's news. You can't dwell on the past because you just set yourself up for a big fall if you do that. Unless you start working towards the next game and trying to improve everything in your own game you'll find other guys leaving you behind.'

LaChapelle admits the Claymores experience rekindled his appetite for football. But that new-found hunger almost landed quarterback Steve Matthews, a team-mate at the Chiefs, in hot water with Jim Criner. 'Coach Criner kept telling Steve early in the season that he had to look to his outlet receivers quicker if I was covered,' said LaChapelle. 'What the coach didn't realise was that I was telling Steve to stay on me no matter what, because I'd get open to make the catch. Poor Steve was getting in trouble for ideas I was having in the huddle.'

To be fair, LaChapelle was rarely bottled up successfully by opposing defences. And nobody suffered more at the hands of LaChapelle than Frankfurt. Even when the gritty receiver risked a badly damaged shoulder to play in the Waldstadion, he delivered the goods as he gave Chris Hall the runaround and grabbed the vital first TD in the fourth quarter.

'That had to be the highlight of the season for me,' he said. 'Sure, I was in pain and one big hit would probably have forced me out of the game, but there was no way I was going to miss out. Steve deserved credit as well because he had to modify every throw. I couldn't raise my right arm above my head so every pass had to come in low and he was bang on the button every time. We had quite a party after that game.'

Sadly for LaChapelle, there was to be no fairytale end to the season. A damaged groin muscle forced him out of the World Bowl action early in the second quarter, before he had any chance to make an impression on the game. LaChapelle admits that at the moment he hit the turf, missing the World Bowl was the least of his worries. 'I just felt something pop in my groin and it was real scary,' he said. 'I've pulled and torn muscles in the past but never felt anything pop the way my groin did.

'My first thought was that I could be finished but the doc reassured me that it wasn't too serious. Once I heard that I was hopeful of getting back out on the field to give the guys a hand but that was ruled out as well. I was so upset because I wanted to do my bit to win the World Bowl for Scotland. In the end they didn't need me because Yo was just sensational and got the plaudits he deserved. It also meant the spotlight was on him, so it wasn't all bad from my point of view!'

WEEK 2: HOMECOMING HEROES
Barcelona Dragons 13 at Scottish Claymores 23

The Claymores were on a mission to bury the ghosts of the season past when they lined up against Jack Bicknell's Barcelona Dragons in week two. Remarkably, none of Bicknell's traditionally high-powered teams had ever lost a regular season game on British soil, but a more pressing statistic for Criner and his new-look Claymores was the fact that the Scots had still to win a match in front of their own supporters at Murrayfield following the five stinging

Defensive end John DeWitt controls the line of scrimmage

Right: Defensive end David Webb in action

George Coghill shuts down the Dragons' offence

home defeats of the 1995 campaign. 'The players who were here last year have reminded everyone about what happened last season,' promised Criner. 'We know what we have to do.'

Heavy rainfall at Stepps had hindered much of the Scots' pre-game preparations and to compound the lack of practice there was a distinct threat to contend with in the arm of Dragons quarterback Kelly Holcomb, who had passed for a team-record 420 yards in Barcelona's impressive 34–21 opening week victory over highly fancied pre-season favourites, Amsterdam Admirals. In order to win, the Claymores hard-hitting defensive line – featuring Troy Ridgley, Ty Parten, Herman Carroll, David Webb and John DeWitt – would have to shut down Holcomb's air attack.

It was to be an important day for Gavin Hastings too, making his Murrayfield debut in helmet and shoulder pads, in his return to a stadium that carried with it so many glorious memories. The former Scotland rugby captain kicked the game off in front of the 12,928 crowd and it wasn't long before they were cheering again as Dragons running back Charles Thompson fumbled the ball on Barcelona's first possession, setting the Claymores up in a great field position.

Paul McCallum's 34-yard field goal gave the Scots a 3–0 lead with four minutes gone before Siran Stacy, behind the solid blocking of full-back Jared Kaaiohelo, powered the Claymores into scoring range on six punishing run plays at the start of the second quarter. Quarterback Steve Matthews picked up where he left off against London, throwing a 12-yard touchdown pass to Sean LaChapelle.

Hastings's extra point made it 10–0 before the Claymores defence made their presence felt, Webb, Parten and Carroll all pressuring Holcomb before he could find an open receiver, forcing the Dragons to punt at the half-time two-minute warning. McCallum kicked another field goal – this time from 38 yards, after LaChapelle made his way out of bounds to stop the clock on a 35-yard pass from Matthews – to make it 13–0 on the stroke of half-time.

McCallum moved the Claymores further in front with a 39-yard field goal at the start of the third quarter, but the Dragons hit back on their next possession when receiver Kenny Shedd hauled in a 57-yard touchdown pass from Holcomb. Scott Szeredy's PAT made it 16–7 and Barcelona were back in the game. But Matthews, who was to finish the day with an impressive 211 yards passing, shifted the momentum back the Claymores' way, firing a 22-yard shot to tight end Willy Tate. Wide receiver Yo Murphy then came up with one of his trademark acrobatic catches, latching on to the end of Matthews's 42-yard bomb which placed the Claymores at the Dragons' two-yard line. One way to make sure points would go on the board would be to hand it to Stacy, and that's just what Jim Criner called. The half-back powered over from two yards to hammer home the Claymores' advantage. Hastings's second PAT gave Scotland a 23–7 lead.

The Dragons were now forced to go exclusively air-borne – the Claymores' stingy defence had limited them to only 13 yards rushing, stifling star running back Terry Wilburn to minus three yards on the ground. However, the do-or-die strategy paid off when Holcomb found tight end Bryce Burnett on a four-yard touchdown pass. But Barcelona's two-point attempt failed when Claymores safety George Coghill broke up Holcomb's pass. The Scots front four then pinned back their ears to pressure Holcomb further and the Dragons could not respond leaving Stacy to run out the clock for the Claymores' first ever victory at Murrayfield by 23–13.

Afterwards Jim Criner made a bold statement: 'We promised a better team this season and we showed that today. If we continue to play the way we did today we've got a great chance of making a run at the whole thing.'

WEEK 2: BARCELONA DRAGONS at SCOTTISH CLAYMORES; MURRAYFIELD, EDINBURGH; 21 APRIL 1996; ATT: 12,928; WEATHER: CLOUDY, 12°C

SCORE BY PERIODS

	1	2	3	4	
DRAGONS	0	0	7	6	13
CLAYMORES	3	10	10	0	23

SCORING SUMMARY

Team	Period	Elapsed Time	Play	Score
Sco	1st	4:07	FG, McCallum 34	0-3
Sco	2nd	6:42	TD, LaChapelle 12 pass Matthews (Hastings PAT)	0-10
Sco	2nd	15:00	FG, McCallum 38	0-13
Sco	3rd	3:46	FG, McCallum 39	0-16
Bar	3rd	6:23	TD, Shedd 57 pass Holcomb (Szeredy PAT)	7-16
Sco	3rd	14:57	TD, Stacy 2 run (Hastings PAT)	7-23
Bar	4th	9:41	TD, Burnett 4 pass Holcomb (2PAT failed)	13-23

TEAM STATISTICS

	DRAGONS	CLAYMORES
First Downs	13	16
Rushes/Yards	11/13	36/85
Net Passing Yards	238	206
Total Net Yards	251	291
Passing (A-C-I)	45/26/3	25/17/1
Punts/Average	5/41.4	5/34.2
Fumbles/Lost	3/1	2/1
Penalties	7/32	5/35
Time of Possession	26:14	33:46

INDIVIDUAL STATISTICS

RUSHING
Dragons: Thompson 8-16; Holcomb 1-0; Edge 1-0; Wilburn 1-(-3)
Claymores: Stacy 26-55-1; Matthews 4-2; Kaaiohelo 2-4; Dickerson 4-24

PASSING
Dragons: Holcomb 44-26-254, 2TD, 0INT; Sacca 1-0-0
Claymores: Matthews 25-17-211, 1TD, 1INT

RECEIVING
Dragons: Davis 7-53; Thompson 3-6; Marshall 2-11; Burnett 8-63-1; Browning 4-49; Shedd 1-57; Wilburn 1-15
Claymores: Bennetts 1-8; Dickerson 2-10; Stacy 4-16; Tate 3-61; Kaaiohelo 1-3; LaChapelle 5-71-1; Murphy 1-42

TY PARTEN/DAVID WEBB: THE DOGS OF WAR

Put two wild dogs in a cage and chances are they'll tear each other apart. Turn those wild dogs loose and they'll chew up anything that gets in their way.

That was the strategy employed by defensive line coach Bill Dutton as he prepared his men for the task ahead at training camp in Atlanta. Dutton's defensive line was put on a leash during their final scrimmage game, with strict orders to give nothing away about the Claymores' defensive strategy. The result? A stomping by Amsterdam in that scrimmage game and a defensive line which arrived in Scotland with bruised egos and a burning desire to prove a point to their World League rivals.

For the next ten weeks, opposition quarterbacks fled in fear as Dutton's dogs of war snapped at their heels. None were fiercer than former college football rivals Ty Parten and David Webb. First round draft pick Parten, a 27-year-old from Scottsdale, Arizona, was eventually voted Defensive Player of the Year, despite playing only six games in the season due to a recurring knee problem. But he insists Webb was the crazy man of the defensive line: 'I knew Webb was completely nuts from our college games and if anything he'd got even crazier by the time he reached Scotland. When I played for Arizona against USC I came up against Webb on special teams. We were both down on the line of scrimmage and I was staring straight at a guy with a Lone Ranger mask painted on his face under his helmet. It was Webb. I made some comment about his mask, he shot back with a comment about my long

Joe O'Brien, Ty Parten and Herman Carroll in the huddle

hair and that was it – war! The ball was snapped and we were both racing downfield, beating the living hell out of each other. I'll tell you what, when I came to training camp I was delighted to find Webb was on my side. He's one mean dude on a football field.'

While Webb was the wild man, Parten left his own impression on more than one quarterback during the season. He admits there is no greater pleasure in football for him than making the big hit. 'Some of those quarterbacks who played against us must have been in the ice tub for days after,' he said. 'We might not have recorded as many sacks as some teams, but sacks only look impressive on the stats sheets.

'The vital thing is getting a hit on the quarterback to shake him up a bit. If he's just got a pass off and he gets nailed he feels it and he's pretty beat up afterwards. A lot of times this season there were four of us hitting the guy at once and that's got to hurt. Herman Carroll and myself would nail him from one side while Webb and Joe O'Brien or John DeWitt would clobber him from the other side. That's no fun if you're a quarterback.' While Parten took the plaudits, the role of Webb and the other defensive linemen should never be underestimated.

Remarkably, Webb played for the 1995 Claymores as a linebacker before bulking up and making the switch to the trenches. He admits the war zone on the line of scrimmage is much more his style of football. 'It was just great in there,' he said. 'The Claymores' defensive line was just like a pack of wild dogs who had been unchained and were snapping and snarling.

'But nobody should forget that we came through a lot of adversity to get the job done. Ty and Herman both got injured in week two and Ty spent the next two weeks on the sidelines. Then the two of them had to fly home after week eight because their knees were damaged. We also lost John DeWitt for a week with food poisoning and I was out for two weeks with an ankle problem. That forced every defensive player to step up and play tough, but there was never any doubt they would. They were a real tough bunch of guys and no matter who was in there, the job got done.'

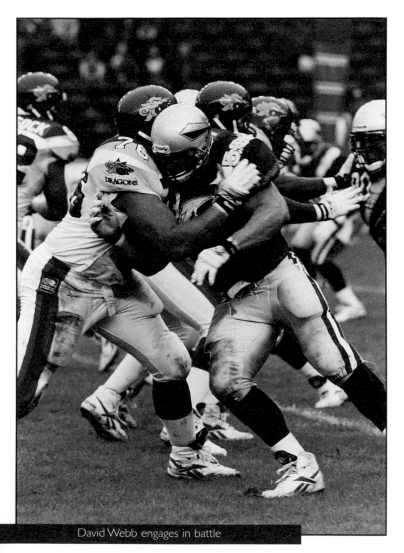
David Webb engages in battle

Webb, from Long Beach, California, had another reason for wanting to make his mark with the Claymores this season. He needed the cash to pay for his wedding. 'I had hoped to marry my fiancée Kelly last year,' he said, 'but I just didn't make enough money with the Claymores. The problem was that I got injured so I didn't get as much playing time as I had hoped for. This year I was determined to impress coach Criner so he couldn't leave me sitting on the bench. I think I was pretty successful and I had a real ball doing it!'

WEEK 3: COUPER ADDS THE TARTAN TOUCH
Amsterdam Admirals 14 at Scottish Claymores 21

The news was not good for the Claymores as they approached one of their biggest tests of the season in week three against the Amsterdam Admirals. Al Luginbill's hostile raiding party had humiliated the Scots the previous season, recording a 31–0 shut-out at Murrayfield before inflicting a 30–13 defeat at their home fortress in Amsterdam's Olympish Stadion. Luginbill hadn't let up in the pre-season either, fielding his strongest possible line-up to run over the Scots 35–10 in their final 'warm-up scrimmage' in Atlanta.

Upsetting that trend would be difficult enough for Criner's revamped and revitalised squad – even after their magnificent start to the season – but they would now have to lay the Dutch bogey to rest without their No.1 draft pick, Ty Parten, and star defensive end Herman Carroll, who had both suffered knee ligament injuries during the victory over the Dragons.

As Parten and Carroll waited for the results of MRI (Magnetic Resonance Imaging) tests Criner, and line coach Bill Dutton, attempted to patch together a makeshift front four. Joe O'Brien, David Webb, John DeWitt and Troy Ridgley would have to match-up to the biggest offensive line in the league – without the luxury of being able to take a breather. 'This has been one we've been looking forward to for a long time,' said coach Criner. 'It's going to be a real barn-burner of a game. Because of our injury situation, our guys on the defensive line are facing long periods on the field without substitution.'

Criner knew early dominance – and a quick score from the offence – would be crucial to take some of the heat off the defence. And the coach got the start he had hoped for, when Siran Stacy cut through the Admirals defence on a nine-yard touchdown run to cap a 12-play opening drive. But the Admirals defence made amends at the end of the first quarter when Bobby Hamilton pressured Steve Matthews forcing a high pass from the quarterback as he attempted to complete to Stacy in the flats. There was nothing but open field between Rico Mack and the endzone as the Admirals' linebacker scooped up Matthews's tipped pass and sprinted 90 yards for a stunning score. A dramatic start, but all that was about to be eclipsed with the emergence of a local hero.

The trials and tribulations of ten years in the amateur leagues followed by a daunting season spent largely on the sidelines trying to grasp the complexities of the professional game were about to bear fruit for former Glasgow Lion Scott Couper. Couper thought his chance of glory had escaped when, after receivers coach Vince Alcalde called his number on a corner pattern, the ball slipped through his hands in the endzone. But No. 81's dream could not be denied when, on third-and-goal, fellow receiver Yo Murphy was sent ahead on a clearing pattern for the young Scot who ran underneath the coverage to make a glorious reception of Matthews's five-yard pass and score his first touchdown as a Claymore.

Couper was to explain afterwards: 'When I saw the ball coming towards me all I could think was: "Catch it! Catch it!" When I turned it was like the parting of the Red Sea in front of me and I was in the end-zone.' The 13,070 fans inside Murrayfield, including Couper's family and friends in the West Stand, went wild with delight as the Claymores bench cleared to celebrate the lightweight national's ground-breaking catch – and the Scots went into the break with their confidence brimming, 14–7 in front.

Luginbill turned to the trick-play section in his playbook at the start of the third quarter after the Claymores defence had held his misfiring offence to a fourth down at their own 27-yard line. Instead of punting the ball it was snapped to cornerback Kelly Sims, who sped from his up-back position, untouched, 73-yards downfield for a game-tying touchdown.

Amsterdam couldn't add to their score in the remainder of the third quarter with the Scots' defence stifling them series after series and Stacy controlling the clock offensively as he pounded out the yards *en route* to his 153-yard total for the day. With two minutes gone in the fourth

GAME STATISTICS

WEEK 3: AMSTERDAM ADMIRALS at SCOTTISH CLAYMORES; MURRAYFIELD, EDINBURGH; 28 APRIL 1996; ATT: 13,070; WEATHER: P/CLOUDY, 12°C

SCORE BY PERIODS

	1	2	3	4	
ADMIRALS	7	0	7	0	14
CLAYMORES	7	7	0	7	21

SCORING SUMMARY

Team	Period	Elapsed Time	Play	Score
Sco	1st	5:43	TD, Stacy 9 run (Hastings PAT)	0-7
Ams	1st	15:00	TD, Mack 90 interception (Werdekker PAT)	7-7
Sco	2nd	10:50	TD, Couper 5 pass Matthews (Hastings PAT)	7-14
Ams	3rd	1:34	TD, Sims 73 run (Werdekker PAT)	14-14
Sco	4th	1:59	TD, Matthews 10 run (Hastings PAT)	14-21

TEAM STATISTICS

	ADMIRALS	CLAYMORES
First Downs	17	18
Rushes/Yards	21/134	38/174
Net Passing Yards	176	126
Total Net Yards	310	300
Passing (A-C-I)	35/20/2	27/16/1
Punts/Average	5/36.9	6/38.0
Fumbles/Lost	3/1	2/2
Penalties	6/40	3/22
Time of Possession	27:00	33:00

INDIVIDUAL STATISTICS

RUSHING
Admirals: Temming 4-8; Cobb 6-12; Furrer 2-10; Bryant 8-31; Sims 1-73-1
Claymores: Stacy 31-153-1; Dickerson 3-4; Thomas 206; Kaaiohelo 1-1; Matthews 1-10-1

PASSING
Admirals: Furrer 34-19-186, 0TD, 2INT; Sacca 1-1-0, 0TD, 0INT
Claymores: Matthews 27-16-146, 1TD, 1INT

RECEIVING
Admirals: Jones 4-62; Hill 4-34; Mack 1-0; Bobo 6-60; Temming 2-1; Smith 2-31; Bryant 1-(-2)
Claymores: Tate 4-35; Dickerson 2-10; LaChapelle 5-51; Couper 1-5-1; Kaaiohelo 1-17; Stacy 1-6; Gissendaner 2-22

quarter, Jim Criner resorted to his own brand of trickery in an attempt to sink the Admirals. Setting up from the sweep, with Stacy powering the Scots into scoring range, Matthews faked to full-back Markus Thomas before bootlegging himself in the opposite direction on a ten-yard touchdown run. Gavin Hastings added to his two previous extra points and the Claymores took a 21–14 lead.

Admirals passer Will Furrer went to the air attempting to salvage the day for the Dutch, but the Claymores defence – boosted with the heroic second-half return of ironman end Herman Carroll – continued their relentless pursuit. The pressure forced Furrer into an uncharacteristic error and safety David Wilson popped up for his second interception to scuttle any Admirals hopes of a comeback.

SCOTT COUPER: LOCAL HERO

When Scott Couper stood shivering on a bitterly cold day at Stirling University back in November 1994, he could scarcely have believed that 18 months later he would be playing in front of 40,000 screaming fans at Murrayfield. Glasgow Lions star receiver Couper had travelled from his Glasgow home to Stirling to take part in the first ever national player trials. One try-out led to another and before long Couper was pounding out the miles along Cramond foreshore in Edinburgh as one of the select few to satisfy the rigorous demands of the Claymores.

The decision to accept the offer of a place at training camp in Atlanta meant a huge commitment on Couper's part. His studies for a PhD in Organometallic and Polymer

Chemistry at Strathclyde University were put on hold as he pursued his dream of a career in professional American football. Although he made it through training camp he must have wondered if the gamble was worth it as the Claymores lurched from one crisis to another during their first season.

But Couper admits that even in those dark days, he was just astonished the Claymores had taken any national players on board. 'To be honest, I thought the national player trials were just a publicity stunt,' he said. 'I went along to Stirling convinced the World League guys would just pitch up, go through the motions and then head off and we'd never hear from them again. I figured they had to keep the amateur players in this country sweet if they hoped to get a decent support at the games and that's what they were doing. I was completely and utterly wrong and I have never been so pleased to be wrong in my entire life.'

Couper scores his first World League touchdown

Couper's rise from the wide-eyed innocent who arrived at training camp in Atlanta to a potent threat at wide receiver in just two seasons has been sensational. Head coach Jim Criner describes Couper's blossoming stature within the game as 'the boy becoming a man'. And the final pay-off for Criner and his coaching staff came as Couper claimed his first ever touchdown against the Admirals. 'I just couldn't believe it when I caught that ball, turned round and saw there was nobody to stop me taking it into the endzone,' said Couper.

'It was the moment I had dreamed about ever since I hooked up with the Claymores. You try and picture what you'll do, how you'll react, when the moment finally arrives, but all my plans went out of the window. Forget touchdown dances, I just lost it completely. My sister was in tears up in the stand and my parents and friends were all standing and cheering. It was a moment which will live with me for ever.'

While that touchdown marked Couper's arrival as a fully paid-up

member of the wide receivers club, he rubber-stamped his right to be in there with the big boys with superb catches throughout the season. None was more impressive than his second TD, a blinding reception in Barcelona. It was a catch hailed on Fox TV as being 'of NFL standard' but to the man himself it was just another day at the office. 'It was lovely to hear what had been said about the touchdown on TV but, honestly, I've made catches like that before. I scored an identical touchdown for the Glasgow Lions. The only difference that day was that there were about 300 people there. This time millions saw it on telly.'

Couper may remain cool about his on-field exploits but his celebrations in the endzone told a different story. 'I lost it again,' he admitted. 'Honestly, after the way I carried on when I scored at Murrayfield I'd promised myself it would be different if I ever scored another touchdown. But all the self-control went again when I picked myself up and realised I'd come up with the ball in the endzone. I think coach Criner dreads the thought of me ever scoring again!'

Couper finally completed his PhD during the 1996 season. But he admits the highlight of his life came a fortnight after that academic achievement when he ran out at Murrayfield for the World Bowl. 'I've been fortunate enough to do well at university and a couple of years ago I probably imagined it would be the highlight of my life to graduate,' he said. 'But playing for the Claymores in the World Bowl eclipsed everything I have ever achieved.

'To win a championship in front of 40,000 of your countrymen is something which makes you feel so proud and it's a chance few Scots will ever get. That day at Murrayfield was unforgettable but so was the whole season. In my first season I felt I was only used in no-risk situations. This season my number was being called on vital third-down plays and I really felt I was contributing to the team. That was a lovely feeling and it's one I hope to sample again next season.'

Couper is confident the crowds will come flocking to Murrayfield next season after the World Bowl extravaganza. 'Look at the viewing figures the television coverage of our games get in this country,' he said. 'Those figures prove there is a huge potential for the sport. A lot of people who maybe saw their first game of American football at the World Bowl will have enjoyed the whole experience and will come back again.

'To think that when I started out in the amateur game people thought I was crazy and going through some sort of phase. That all seems such a long time ago now.'

WEEK 4: CONTROVERSY SENDS RECORD UP IN FLAMES
Scottish Claymores 14 at Rhein Fire 15

With Frankfurt Galaxy the only other unbeaten team going into week four, the Claymores' visit to Dusseldorf to face winless Rhein Fire had become irrelevant to the outcome of the first half of the season. The following week's match-up in the Waldstadion between the Scots and the reigning World League champions Galaxy would now determine the winners of the first half of the regular season, and, with it, the right to host World Bowl 96. However, Jim Criner was aware that victory over Galen Hall's Rhein Fire – who had lost narrowly to Frankfurt in week one and were still chasing their first victory of the season – would be crucial in sustaining his team's drive for that week-five showdown. 'I know they are going to give us their best shot,' said Criner. 'But you win championships on the road, and we really have to dictate the tempo of this game early if we expect to win.'

The defensive line, still without Ty Parten, had been boosted with the return of Claymores veteran Jerold Jeffcoat, just recovered from an injury picked up during the Atlanta training camp. Bryan Proby, the Kansas City Chiefs allocated defensive end who had suffered an abdominal injury in the pre-season, had now also flown to Scotland to join the squad.

But a pre-match mix-up, when the driver assigned by Rhein Fire to take the visiting Scots to the stadium on the afternoon of the match took a wrong turning, was a portent for things to come as the Claymores aimed to maintain their unbeaten run. Arriving late at the stadium, the players barely had time to don their uniforms before kick-off and the lack of composure showed on the field as Rhein shot out to a surprise lead when quarterback Andy Kelly fired a 21-yard touchdown pass to tight end Byron Chamberlain on the German's opening drive.

The Claymores' defence weren't the only ones having problems settling, with quarterback Steve Matthews finding it difficult to get his offence moving. However, the passer, who was to finish the day with a disappointing 16 completions from 27 attempts, finally managed to link up with Siran Stacy on a screen pass – the rusher jinking around three tacklers on his way to a 21-yard touchdown score. Gavin Hastings kicked the PAT and, despite the early adversity, the Claymores were up 7–6.

But misfortune continued to dog the Scots, robbing them of the chance to capitalise on the lead at the start of the second quarter. A poor refereeing call handed possession back to Rhein after the Claymores looked to have recovered a muffed punt return and, eight plays later, Rhein kicker Leo Araguz converted a 39-yard field goal for a 9–7 half-time lead,

before making it 12–7 with another field goal – this time from 33 yards – at the start of the third.

Receiver Sean LaChapelle got the Claymores back into contention at the start of the final period, making a stunning touchdown catch in between two defenders from a 32-yard Matthews pass. However, instead of opting for two points Criner sent on Hastings. The kicker made

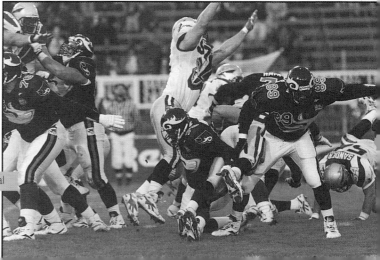

Claymores defence attempts to block a Fire field goal

GAME STATISTICS

WEEK 4: SCOTTISH CLAYMORES at RHEIN FIRE; RHEINSTADION, DUSSELDORF; 4 MAY 1996; ATT: 11,395; WEATHER: CLOUDY, 10°C

SCORE BY PERIODS

	1	2	3	4	
CLAYMORES	7	0	0	7	14
RHEIN FIRE	6	3	3	3	15

SCORING SUMMARY

Team	Period	Elapsed Time	Play	Score
Rhe	1st	2:59	TD, Chamberlain 21 pass Kelly	0-6
Sco	1st	11:59	TD, Stacy 21 pass Matthews (Hastings PAT)	7-6
Rhe	2nd	9:30	FG, Araguz 39	7-9
Rhe	3rd	13:14	FG, Araguz 33	7-12
Sco	4th	0:44	TD, LaChapelle 32 pass Matthews (Hastings PAT)	14-12
Rhe	4th	7:03	FG, Araguz 23	14-15

TEAM STATISTICS

	CLAYMORES	RHEIN FIRE
First Downs	11	13
Rushes/Yards	23/83	28/87
Net Passing Yards	156	172
Total Net Yards	239	259
Passing (A-C-I)	27/16/0	31/20/1
Punts/Average	8/35.6	5/39.8
Fumbles/Lost	3/1	3/0
Penalties	7/45	4/25
Time of Possession	25:34	34:26

INDIVIDUAL STATISTICS

RUSHING
Claymores: Stacy 16-54; Matthews 4-7; Dickerson 2-13; Thomas 1-9
Fire: Richardson 5-19; Clark 10-37; Carter 3-3; Kelly 5-1; Davison 5-27

PASSING
Claymores: Matthews 27-16-170, 2TD, 0INT
Fire: Kelly 31-20-177, 1TD, 1INT

RECEIVING
Claymores: Stacy 6-32-1; LaChapelle 6-97-1; Kaaiohelo 1-6; Murphy 1-9; Tate 1-21; Coghill 1-5
Fire: Boyd 2-35; Chamberlain 3-52-1; Davison 1-4; Clark 10-57; Richardson 2-8; Knox 1-11; Woods 1-10

the PAT and the Scots held a slender 14–12 advantage. That lead was wiped out when Araguz, having a field day, nailed a 23-yard kick to put Fire back in front at 15–14.

The Claymores had to punt on their next possession but with 1:41 still left the Scots were set to get one last chance of a comeback as the defence held Kelly's attack to a crucial third-and-three. The Rhein quarterback threw his pass, intended for receiver Kevin Knox, incomplete – which should have been enough to send on the punt team – but during the course of the play line judge Boris Cheek stumbled and fell to the ground. Thinking he may have been tripped, Cheek threw a flag calling an unsportsmanlike penalty against the Claymores' sideline, handing an automatic first down to Rhein Fire which allowed them to run out the clock in front of the 11,395 home support for their first win, and the Claymores' first loss, of the season.

Somehow managing to retain his diplomacy afterwards, a bemused Jim Criner said: 'I didn't agree with the call. Usually the officials will notify us if our players are getting too close to the field but I received zero complaints and then, all of a sudden, we get a flag. I really don't understand it, to be honest with you.'

MARK SANDER: THE LOUISVILLE SLUGGER

If you had asked Claymores defensive captain Mark Sander where he felt happiest during the Claymores' championship season, he'd have told you: 'On the football field.' It's true that like his father – an Oklahoma cowboy – the former Miami Dolphins starting linebacker loves to ride his horse, play poker and listen to his favourite brand of country music anytime he's back down on his farm in Louisville, Kentucky, the home of the famous horse-racing derby – a fact Sander is always proud to remind you of. But it was on the gridiron, and more specifically in the middle of the field, where this self-confessed 'hard-nosed' Claymore – nicknamed 'Big Country' by his team-mates – felt most relaxed this year.

Sander, who was second on the Claymores defence with 51 bone-crunching tackles and two sacks, is a throwback to the hard-hitting, bloody-nosed, mud and guts, golden era of NFL and AFL line-backing of the 1950s and 1960s. And along with legendary linebackers Chuck Bednarik, Sam Huff and Dick Butkus, Sander shares one common interest: he likes to hit. 'I love playing football and I love the middle-linebacker position,' said the 28-year-old defensive captain, whose quiet demeanour off the field is at opposite poles to his approach on it. 'I like to be in the thick of things in there and, most of all, to do some hitting.'

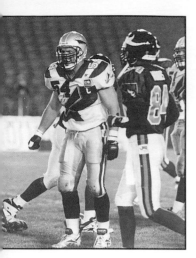

But don't be fooled by what Sander says. Along with his penchant for high impacts, the University of Louisville graduate, who spent three years in the NFL – two with the Dan Marino-led Dolphins – also displayed the intelligence crucial in mastering the key position at the heart of the Claymores' World Bowl winning defence. 'The middle linebacker is the quarterback of the defence,' explained Sander. 'He calls the plays and makes the adjustments, so it is not just a matter of brute force. You have to be thinking in there as well.'

This fact is not lost on Sander's coaches, who had entrusted the Claymores' captaincy for the last two seasons to the experience and intelligence of the hard-hitting University of Louisville slugger. 'Mark Sander was our defensive general who held the whole thing together for us this season,' said Claymores head coach Jim Criner. 'He is a complete professional,' added linebackers' coach Larry Owens. 'He's a young man who is very, very intelligent. He loves the game, he plays hard, he practises hard and he does all the things you would expect a professional athlete to do. He, in my opinion, was the leader of our football team this year. He held the linebackers together while going about his own job.'

It was a role that Sander, one of only a handful of players invited back to the Claymores this season by Criner, was honoured to assume. 'I do have a responsibility as a team leader but I'm quite happy to take that on if the coaches have confidence in me to do it. To be honest, I'm just happy to be back playing football here in Scotland.'

Playing professional football is something Sander thought he would never do again after being dropped by the Dolphins 'for younger blood' three years ago. He then suffered the indignity of sitting out of football for two years before the revival of the World League in 1995 gave him a second chance. 'It was a very frustrating time for me,' admitted the linebacker: 'I was back home watching NFL football telling myself, "I'm good enough to be out there. Why aren't I out there?" I was told that I wasn't good enough and wasn't needed right now, but deep inside my heart I knew I was good enough to play so I just kept plugging away to get back in. That's why the World League is such a great thing. It gives players like me, who've just missed out, a second shot at it. That's why I first came to Scotland.

'But this year things were a little different. I didn't hold out much hope of getting back into the NFL at the start of the season. I think this year was more a case of giving something back to the fans in Scotland. I wanted to win so badly for them and for me – I had never won a title before we won the World Bowl for Scotland. I know the national players we have on the team very well – Ben Torriero and Scott Couper – and I know how much it meant to them.'

It's perhaps fitting that one of Sander's favourite songs is *A Country Boy Can Survive* by Hank Williams Jnr. Sander has managed not only to survive in the tough world of professional football, but has excelled in the World League. So much so, that, despite the linebacker's pessimistic prediction, he has earned a return to the NFL – signed shortly after the World Bowl victory to the famous San Francisco 49ers. 'Compared to last year it was 100 per cent improvement,' said Sander. 'You've got to remember that Coach Criner took over in the first week of last season and wasn't able to assemble the team that he might have wanted.

'However, this year he was in charge from the get-go and brought in three good defensive coaches in Ray Willsey, Bill Dutton and Larry Owens. The result of this was that we were able to enjoy playing some hard defence this season – and ultimately won the World Bowl with it. From the start of the season we made it our aim to host the World Bowl. Defensively we just stoked it up in those first five games and through hard work we realised our ambition.

'We were a class defence – we didn't get involved in trash-talking or dirty play – but throughout the season you could see how hard we hit because the teams we played against always had a lot of injuries and usually lost the following week. That's what the name of the game is on defence, and that's what we proved this season in winning the World Bowl.'

WEEK 5: FROM THE OUTHOUSE TO THE PENTHOUSE
Scottish Claymores 20 at Frankfurt Galaxy 0

The Claymores had come a long way from those dark days of '95 when they suffered the humiliation of defeat and the label of the World League's worst team. Now, in week five of the '96 season, the Claymores had turned 180 degrees and were facing the biggest game in their short history.

All that had to be done to clinch the first half of the season, and with it the right to host World Bowl 96 at Murrayfield, was to fly to Frankfurt and defeat the reigning and unbeaten World League champions Galaxy – featuring the high-powered offence of league-leading quarterback Steve Pelluer – in front of their own support, a hostile crowd of around 32,000 screaming Germans in the awesome Waldstadion.

It was a tall order for any team at any time but with the injury situation not getting any better – stand-out wide receiver Sean LaChapelle, full-back Ron Dickerson and centre Lance Zeno were all doubtful, injured during the morale-sapping loss in Dusseldorf the previous week – it was beginning to look like *Mission Impossible* for Jim Criner and his Claymores, with the odds stacked up against them.

To compound the difficulties, Criner was forced to release veteran defensive tackle Troy Ridgley and quarterback Terry Karg, both solid servants of the Claymores since the club's inception, and safety Marvin Goodwin just three days before the showdown in Frankfurt. With players like Ty Parten and cornerback Forey Duckett coming off the injured reserve list it was inevitable that someone would have to go to make room on the roster, but so close to this most important of matches the danger was that team cohesion could suffer.

Despite having to make some tough decisions, Criner was still positive in the run-up to the game, saying: 'The opportunity to host the World Bowl is something we are all excited about and I feel we have a good chance to win in Frankfurt.' To do so, the Claymores' top-rated defence would somehow have to stop former Dallas Cowboys passer Pelluer from linking up with the league's top-rated receiving corps of Jay Kearney, Gary Harrell, Mike Bellamy and Mario Bailey, who had all combined to down a strong Amsterdam 40–28 the previous week, making Galaxy the league's most potent offence with 137 points scored in just four games. But in the end, it was Ray Willsey's stingy and hard-hitting defence that proved the most powerful weapon.

GAME STATISTICS

WEEK 5: SCOTTISH CLAYMORES at FRANKFURT GALAXY;
WALDSTADION, FRANKFURT; 11 MAY 1996; ATT: 32,126; WEATHER:
SUNNY, 12°C

SCORE BY PERIODS

	1	2	3	4	
CLAYMORES	3	0	3	14	20
GALAXY	0	0	0	0	0

SCORING SUMMARY

Team	Period	Elapsed Time	Play	Score
Sco	1st	13:14	FG, McCallum 32	3-0
Sco	3rd	14:33	FG, McCallum 25	6-0
Sco	4th	5:37	TD, LaChapelle 21 pass Matthews (Hastings PAT)	13-0
Sco	4th	10:11	TD, Thomas 3 run (Hastings PAT)	20-0

TEAM STATISTICS

	CLAYMORES	GALAXY
First Downs	19	13
Rushes/Yards	35/162	17/83
Net Passing Yards	261	127
Total Net Yards	423	210
Passing (A-C-I)	21/15/0	39/19/5
Punts/Average	5/32	6/35.3
Fumbles/Lost	2/2	0
Penalties	3/14	4/25
Time of Possession	32:18	27:42

INDIVIDUAL STATISTICS

RUSHING
Claymores: Stacy 25-133; Kaaiohelo 3-10; Matthews 5-11; Thomas 2-8-1
Galaxy: Bolton 3-1; Seibert 4-17; Phillips 8-44; Pelluer 1-(-1); Bretz 1-22

PASSING
Claymores: Matthews 21-15-261, 1TD, 0INT
Galaxy: Pelluer 15-5-60, 0TD, 2INT; Bretz 24-14-100, 0TD, 3INT

RECEIVING
Claymores: LaChapelle 6-180-1; Kaaiohelo 2-0; Couper 2-10; Stacy 3-23; Murphy 2-48;
Galaxy: Bailey 5-56; Kearney 4-48; Harrell 1-5; Phillips 3-5; Bellamy 5-46; Seibert 1-0

MID-SEASON STANDINGS (AFTER FIVE GAMES)

	W	L	T	PCT	PF	PA
Scottish Claymores*	4	1	0	.800	102	63
Frankfurt Galaxy	4	1	0	.800	137	101
Barcelona Dragons	3	2	0	.600	106	99
Amsterdam Admirals	2	3	0	.400	114	111
London Monarchs	1	4	0	.200	67	118
Rhein Fire	1	4	0	.200	82	106

* Qualified for World Bowl 96 as first-half winners on head-to-head tie-breaker against Frankfurt

Like all good cup finals the game was a tense affair with both offences finding it difficult to put together any sustained attack in the first half. However, it was the underdog Claymores who looked more confident as Pelluer found it impossible to get into any type of groove, under constant pressure from the Scots' front four. The Claymores offence had chances to mark up touchdowns – with Siran Stacy doing the bulk of the work *en route* to a 133-yard rushing performance – but could only manage two Paul McCallum field goals – from 32 and 25 yards – to post a 6–0 lead early in the third quarter.

Despite great play from the line, the night was to belong to a player from the defensive backfield. Former Galaxy safety James Fuller, cut by Frankfurt head coach Ernie Stautner in the pre-season, was about to come back to haunt his old side in the blue and white of a Claymores uniform. Fuller popped up to give the Galaxy quarterbacks nightmares with two key interceptions in the third and fourth quarters. Fellow defensive backs James Williams, Forey Duckett and George Coghill also came up with key interceptions as the Scots' defensive line made life a misery for Pelluer and his replacement quarterback Brad Bretz.

Fittingly, it was another

interception, this time from linebacker Arnold Ale, after defensive captain Mark Sander had popped the ball loose, hitting Mario Bailey as he attempted to make a catch, which broke Galaxy's back. Four plays later Sean LaChapelle broke free on a glorious post pattern to extend the Claymores' lead, catching Steve Matthews's 21-yard pass in the endzone. Gavin Hastings added the PAT to make it 13–0. But it might as well have been 30–0 as the once mighty Galaxy folded at the Claymores' feet. Fuller's second interception – of a deep Bretz pass as he attempted to find Bailey – followed on Frankfurt's next possession and nailed the lid shut on any German comeback. Fuller

Randy Bierman blocks his man

Siran Stacy surrounded by the Galaxy

explained afterwards: 'I had something to prove over here and thankfully it worked out the way I wanted, but I was playing within a bigger system and our line did a great job of getting to their passer.'

Matthews drove his team downfield once more and running back Markus Thomas capped the drive with a three-yard saunter into the endzone. Hastings's second PAT brought the score to 20–0 before the defence brought the proceedings to a close, George Coghill's safety blitz sacking Bretz to maintain the Scots' shutout and ice a remarkable night for the Claymores.

'Everyone here tonight feels we've done something for Scotland,' said Gavin Hastings afterwards. 'It really feels great to be part of this and there's no reason now why we can't fill Murrayfield with over 40,000 fans for the World Bowl.' Coach Criner, vindicated after the agonies of '95, echoed his kicker's statement, saying: 'This is a great victory for us but also a great victory for Scotland. Bringing the World Bowl to Murrayfield is a great way to thank our fans for everything they had to go through last year. We've gone from the outhouse to the penthouse, and it feels great.'

JAMES FULLER: A MAN ON A MISSION

If it's true that every cloud has a silver lining, James Fuller must have been rained on an awful lot of times in his pro football career. The powerhouse safety from Tacoma must have thought he was made when he was snapped up by the San Diego Chargers in 1992 but injury forced him to sit out the entire season. Even when the 27-year-old made the breakthrough the following year and played ten games it wasn't enough, and he was cut in 1994.

Fuller got his second chance via the New Orleans Saints, being allocated to Frankfurt Galaxy for the 1996 World League season. But for the man who would be head prefect in the school of hard knocks, another crushing setback was lurking around the corner. Despite an excellent training camp in Atlanta, Galaxy head coach Ernie Stautner cut him as he reduced his squad to the required 40 players.

For the first time in his career, Fuller got a break as Jim Criner moved quickly to offer him a chance with the Claymores. It was a move which was to pay real dividends for Criner as Fuller repaid his faith with an outstanding season. No team suffered at his hands more than Frankfurt as Fuller mounted a personal crusade to prove Stautner wrong. That proof was never more in evidence than in the Waldstadion as Fuller and the Claymores clinched the right to host the World Bowl.

Fuller's two interceptions capped an awesome display by the defence as they shut out the highly rated Frankfurt offence. 'I had a real big point to prove against them,' he said. 'As far as I was concerned they were wrong to cut me from their squad so it was personal when I went out on to the field that night. They said I was a victim of the numbers game because they had to reduce the squad in line with the rules of the league but I can't go along with that. I felt I did everything expected of me in training camp so I was pretty bitter at missing out. When I grabbed those two interceptions I celebrated like I've never done before because I wanted them to know how much I was enjoying it. I also wanted their fans to see what they had missed out on because their team decided to cut me.'

Claymores' defensive co-ordinator Ray Willsey memorably insisted after that Frankfurt encounter that Fuller had earned himself the right to 'an easy-chair' after years of finding nothing but hard seats during his football career. But Fuller, who was to notch another four interceptions during the season, including another against Frankfurt in the World Bowl, insisted he's still looking for that easy-chair. 'I don't know about an easy-chair,' he grinned, 'coach Willsey was still working us like dogs the week after that Frankfurt game. But that was the key to our success. There was no magic formula, no short-cut. It was hard work, pure and simple. That, and a tremendous team spirit, was what carried us through. For my part, I felt I owed a great deal to coach Criner and coach Willsey for giving me the chance to be part of their team.'

James Fuller marks his man

Fuller's burning sense of injustice against Frankfurt had him insisting he not only wanted to beat them in the World Bowl, but beat them impressively. But in the cold light of day, as he savoured the achievement, he admits the nail-biting win the Claymores claimed was just as sweet. 'When I was walking around Murrayfield after the game wearing my World Bowl Champions T-shirt, it finally sunk in what we had achieved,' he said. 'So few players get the chance to play in a championship game in their careers and there we were, the best in our league.

'I only really appreciated just how special it was when I saw the faces of the Frankfurt players after the match. The looks on their faces said it all. Their chance had gone for the season. For all I had an axe to grind with Frankfurt for the way they treated me, I had no beef with any of their players. You can't go through a whole training camp with people without forming friendships. But I was so pleased I wasn't a Frankfurt player that night and so proud to be a Scottish Claymore.'

Fuller will take more than footballing memories back to New Orleans with him. Not content with turning in a performance which earned him the honour of Defensive Player of

Fuller and coach Larry Owens celebrate victory in Frankfurt

the Week after his heroics in Frankfurt, Fuller tried his hand at a different skill on the flight home. After learning that linebacker Karmeeleyah McGill had arranged a visit to the flight deck, Fuller decided to go one better. 'I want to land this plane,' he told a stewardess, and while that was ruled out for safety reasons, he was allowed on to the flight deck in time for touchdown at Heathrow. 'That was quite something,' he said. 'I was going around the airport after we landed, asking the guys what they thought of the job I'd done getting the plane down.

'There were all these other people looking and staring when I talked about landing the plane and thinking "This guy's crazy". But I know I was on that flight deck and that's all that matters. In a way, it's a bit like the whole Claymores experience was for me. People kept looking at me as if I was crazy when I said we would win in Frankfurt and host the World Bowl. We all knew we were good enough to go and win it, but there were still people who doubted us. The only people who didn't doubt us were the fans and we didn't let them down.'

WEEK 6: REVENGE OVER RHEIN
Rhein Fire 19 at Scottish Claymores 24

Just when Jim Criner thought all of his troubles were behind him, what was thought to be a flu virus swept through the Claymores' training camp ahead of their week-six rematch with Rhein Fire. Eight starters were hit by the mysterious bug as well as receivers coach Vince Alcalde. It wasn't until after that weekend's match that food poisoning, picked up during the Claymores' victorious visit to Frankfurt, was pinpointed as the true cause of the disruption. Worst hit was defensive end John DeWitt, who would be out for the next three weeks due to the illness, but also hit hard was the offensive line with starters Lance Zeno, Tom Barndt and Matt Storm all suffering.

Criner was perplexed. 'We always seem to get some kind of bad luck when we face Rhein Fire. We never seem to play like we should against them which is why they are still the only team in the league we have never beaten.' And the coach added: 'You hate to hand a team like them any advantage. Our players really wanted to play well against them and I guess now we've got a little added incentive to overcome all the problems. Everyone knows how important it is to keep improving and building right up to the World Bowl.' Defensive end Ty Parten was confident there would be no let-up. 'Call it revenge if you like, but everyone wants another crack at these guys to show that we are No.1 and to keep us on top.'

Canadian Football League quarterback Khari Jones joined the squad to replace Terry Karg, while star receiver Sean LaChapelle would sit the match out on injured reserve. The week-four defeat had shown that Denver Broncos allocated running back Derrick Clark and tight end Byron Chamberlain were Rhein's danger men.

The mark of a championship team is its ability to overcome adversity, and in the first quarter the Claymores certainly looked like world-beaters as running back Siran Stacy led the charge on the Scots' first possession, powering 31 yards behind superb line-blocking and through the middle of Rhein's defence for the first touchdown after only two minutes in front of the 12,419 Murrayfield crowd.

Rhein Fire got on the board when Leo Araguz converted a 29-yard field goal but the Claymores blasted back when Ron Dickerson caught a 20-yard pass from Steve Matthews to set Stacy up for his second score in as many Claymore possessions. Stacy caught Matthews's swing pass and burst 28 yards up the sidelines and into the endzone untouched. Gavin Hastings made amends for missing his first extra point attempt – his 13th of the season – booting through a 29-yard PAT, following a penalty, to give the Claymores a 13–3 lead with just eight minutes gone.

GAME STATISTICS

WEEK 6: RHEIN FIRE at SCOTTISH CLAYMORES; MURRAYFIELD, EDINBURGH; 19 MAY 1996; ATT: 12,419; WEATHER: OVERCAST, 7°C

SCORE BY PERIODS

	1	2	3	4	
RHEIN FIRE	3	3	7	6	19
CLAYMORES	13	11	0	0	24

SCORING SUMMARY

Team	Period	Elapsed Time	Play	Score
Sco	1st	2:01	TD, Stacy 31 run	0-6
Rhe	1st	6:47	FG, Araguz 29	3-6
Sco	1st	8:43	TD, Stacy 28 pass Matthews (Hastings PAT)	3-13
Sco	2nd	0:41	TD, Kaaiohelo 9 run (LaChapelle 2PAT)	3-21
Sco	2nd	5:05	FG, McCallum 25	3-24
Rhe	2nd	12:35	FG, Araguz 28	6-24
Rhe	3rd	12:33	TD, Chamberlain 9 pass Kelly (Burgsmuller PAT)	13-24
Rhe	4th	5:35	TD, Richardson 20 (2PAT failed)	19-24

TEAM STATISTICS

	RHEIN FIRE	CLAYMORES
First Downs	23	15
Rushes/Yards	20/85	28/121
Net Passing Yards	269	178
Total Net Yards	354	299
Passing (A-C-I)	47/28/2	23/13/0
Punts/Average	1/28.0	5/36.0
Fumbles/Lost	1/1	1/1
Penalties	4/20	7/58
Time of Possession	31:52	28:02

INDIVIDUAL STATISTICS

RUSHING

Fire: Richardson 6-36-1; Clark 5-29; Carter 4-9; Davison 3-10; Dean 2-1
Claymores: Stacy 21-75-1; Kaaiohelo 3-9-1; Matthews 3-34; Dickerson 1-3

PASSING

Fire: Kelly 39-25-244, 1TD, 1INT; Dean 8-3-41, 0TD, 1INT
Claymores: Matthews 22-12-130, 1TD, 0INT; Jones 1-1-9, 0TD, 0INT

RECEIVING

Fire: Boyd 2-19; Richardson 4-30; Woods 3-25; Clark 2-10; Chamberlain 8-130-1; Carter 1-15; Davison 7-44; Knox 1-12
Claymores: Dickerson 2-29; Stacy 5-94-1; Couper 1-14; Tate 1-16; Kaaiohelo 1-1; Murphy 2-27; Gissendaner 1-8

Full-back Jared Kaaiohelo scored his first touchdown as a Claymore on the Scots' next possession, powering over from nine yards to cap a nine-play drive at the start of the second period. Matthews completed the two-point conversion to Sean LaChapelle in the corner of the endzone and, after a 25-yard Paul McCallum field goal and a 28-yard reply from Araguz, the Claymores led 24–6 at the half.

Siran Stacy reached a milestone in his World League career with 44 first-half yards to secure the all-time, all-purpose yardage record previously set by Tony Baker of Frankfurt in 1991, thus becoming the league's most productive player ever. But despite Stacy's achievement the Claymores came out flat in the third quarter allowing Rhein to get back into the game. Fire quarterback Andy Kelly directed a 13-play drive which culminated in a nine-yard touchdown pass to Chamberlain and a Burgsmuller PAT to relight Fire's hopes at 24–13.

Scotland's subdued offence couldn't respond and Rhein running back Terry Richardson brought the Germans back to within five points of the lead with five minutes remaining, cutting through a tired Claymores defence on a stunning 20-yard touchdown run. And Fire would have been within a field goal of tying the game if

Herman Carroll hadn't swatted down Kelly's attempted two-point conversion pass, meaning Rhein would now have to score another touchdown to win.

Inspired by Carroll's example the Scots' Braveheart defence rose to the challenge as Kelly moved his team into scoring range on their next possession with another pass – this time for 22 yards – to Chamberlain. With only 29 seconds left it was up to Claymores defensive tackle Jerold Jeffcoat to stop the rot and the veteran did just that, stepping up to make the game's decisive play, sacking Kelly for a 12-yard loss to leave Rhein facing a hopeless fourth down with 27 yards to go. The Fire quarterback desperately tried to find Chamberlain once more but his pass was tipped away by linebacker Shannon Jones allowing the Claymores to turn the tables on their German jinx team, running out the clock 24–19 winners.

'We did everything right in the first half,' commented Claymores safety James Fuller after the match, 'but for some reason the spark was gone when we came back out after the half-time break. In the end the game could have gone either way.' Coach Criner explained: 'I think the events of last week contributed to our second-half problems. We had guys playing who weren't fully fit. But you can rest assured we'll all be up for next week's game when Galaxy come to town.'

GEORGE COGHILL: HATS OFF TO THE HITMAN

Heartbeat. The Hitman. The Hammer. Call him what you like. Just don't let big George Coghill hear you. In a game played by tough men, Coghill is one of the toughest around. A returning Claymore who experienced all the heartache and trauma of the 1995 season, Coghill put those bitter memories to good use as he harnessed all the pent-up frustration of a disastrous year to turn in a powerhouse season. Five interceptions, two Defensive-Player-of-the-Week awards and his first ever MVP award at Murrayfield in week seven against Frankfurt tell their own story. Big George was on fire this season.

Coghill, who graduated in sociology from Wake Forest University, has ambitions to join the FBI or CIA after his football career is over. Heaven help the bad guys if Coghill is on their tail. He racked up 61 tackles in the regular season and every player on the receiving end will testify that when Coghill hits you, you stay hit. Replays of his bone-jarring tackles on the big screen at Murrayfield brought gasps and winces from the Claymores fans.

Coghill is the first to admit he loves every minute of the trench warfare that is American football. 'It's hit or be hit and every one of us out there knows that,' he said. 'There are no prizes for coming second. That's why I'm so proud of the nicknames I've been given. They sound tough, as if people respect your ability to look after yourself and your team-mates on the field and that respect is vital. If people think they can take advantage of you, they'll do it in a second and suddenly you'll be right up against it in a football game. If you get your hit in first you've got them on the back foot and in a contact sport like ours that is so vital.'

The tough guy on the field is one of the nicest off it. But his absolute commitment to winning ensures there are no free gifts being doled out while Coghill is around. 'Sometimes you hit a running back or a wide receiver and you hear a little grunt from him,' he said. 'That's when you know you've done the job right. He's felt that hit and he knows you can hurt him. Maybe next time his number is called he might think twice about stepping into your territory. That's the way you want him to think. You want him to fear you. It doesn't always work; the good players will always come back for more because they don't want you to know you've intimidated them. But if they come back, you've just got to go straight back out there and give them more of the same.'

Coghill admits he doesn't always come out on top in his head-to-head confrontations. But ask him to name his second prizes this season and the 26-year-old's trademark grin lights up his face. 'I took a real big shot against Frankfurt and I think a guy from London nailed me as well,' he said. 'Other than that, I think I did most of the hitting. I got injured once in the season but that was my own fault. I tried to turn too quickly and sprained my ankle, so it's not a bad report card for this term.'

Coghill's hard-hitting doesn't just produce results on defences but also on special teams. It was the safety who gave the Claymores a dream start in the World Bowl, stripping the ball from Mario Bailey on the opening kick-off return to set up Markus Thomas for a touchdown run. 'That's probably the most satisfying play I've ever made,' he said. 'It also proves there's more to this game than brute force. I really didn't hit Bailey very hard at all but I got a good hand on the ball and popped it loose. I was on the ground by the time Markus grabbed the ball but when I heard the crowd roaring I knew it was good news for us.'

Coghill adds another string to his bow with at least one touchdown a season. Last year it was in London. This year he saved his speciality for Murrayfield and the Claymores fans. When Herman Carroll tipped Steve Pelluer's pass Coghill was on it in a flash and returned it 32 yards for a touchdown. 'The touchdowns are a nice little bonus,' he said, 'because defensive players don't pay too many visits to the opposition endzone. When the chance comes you've got to grab it but I don't bother with any of those fancy touchdown dances. I'd look stupid doing something like that and it's not really my style. Although it's nice to get a touchdown now and then, I'll never lose sight of the fact that my main job is to beat 'em up at the other end of the field. That's what I get paid for and it's what I do best.'

That ability to get in where it hurts ensures Coghill's ambitions in the field of law enforcement will remain on hold for now. 'I specialise in building psychological profiles of criminals. That was my chief subject at university. But while I'm still involved with football I won't get much of a chance to use those skills. You can't really join the police for eight months of the year, then tell them you need four months off to play football in Scotland or wherever. That doesn't make for very good career prospects, so for the moment I'm happy to concentrate on playing football.'

George Coghill ready to make his entrance

WEEK 7: McCALLUM HAS A FIELD DAY

Frankfurt Galaxy 17 at Scottish Claymores 20

Frankfurt Galaxy were on a mission when they flew into Scotland for their week-seven rematch with the high-flying Claymores. The German champions had been humilated two weeks before in front of their own fans in the Waldstadion as the Scots handed them their first whitewash in three years, claiming the right to host the World Bowl in a 20–0 triumph.

Galaxy head coach Ernie Stautner was furious after the loss and had wielded his own claymore, sacking offensive co-ordinator Thomas Coleman in reprisal for the defeat. Frankfurt were watching their hopes of winning the second half of the season, and with it

the visitors berth in the Bowl game, disintegrate before their very eyes after suffering a shock defeat to lowly London Monarchs. They now had to start winning if they wanted to have a chance to defend their title.

Jim Criner, with his own goals in mind, was aware of the threat the desperate Germans posed. 'This is a big game for both teams,' said the coach. 'It's really important that we continue our upward progress and sustain our momentum going into the World Bowl. But I know our opponents are going to show up with revenge in mind.' Criner added: 'Since our last meeting they've gone back to basics and simplified their offence, which can sometimes cause you bigger problems, because with less to think about your opponents tend to execute a lot better. Defensively our coaches will have to make sure our players are alert. We are going to have to have one of our best games in order to beat them.'

Paul McCallum must have wondered when he would have his best game as he sliced a 48-yard field goal wide right three minutes into the game. The Canadian Football League kicker, and one-time soccer trialist with St Mirren, was suffering a mid-season slump and was desperate to see his game improve ahead of the World Bowl. Steve Matthews's form seemed to have deserted him too. The quarterback hadn't thrown an interception in three starts but now threw two on consecutive possessions, the second of which was tipped at the line by Don Reynolds and returned 30 yards for the game's opening touchdown by Galaxy safety Chris Hall.

McCallum began to find his range at the start of the second quarter, converting a 28-yard field goal to put the Scots on the scoreboard after tight end Willy Tate's apparent endzone catch was ruled incomplete. However, the kicker missed his second field goal – this time from 32 yards – to end the first half on a low note for the home team, who went into the locker room after a dismal performance trailing visitors Galaxy 7–3. As Jim Criner made his team adjustments at the break McCallum sat alone contemplating his performance, and quietly resolved to make amends.

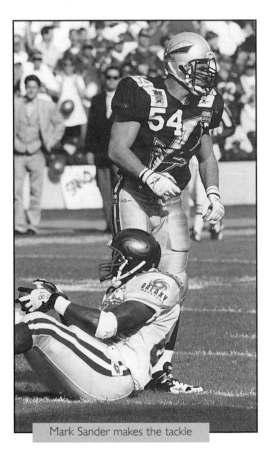
Mark Sander makes the tackle

The Claymores hit fast after the break, wide receiver Sean LaChapelle simply outran cornerback Chris Hall after catching Matthews's pass on a stunning 52-yard touchdown play. Hastings's PAT boosted the Scots to a 10–7 lead. Frankfurt answered back when Ralf Kleinmann converted a 32-yard field goal and it was beginning to look grim for the Claymores when Matthews threw his third interception of the day – picked off by Galaxy safety Johnny Dixon. However, once again the Braveheart defence stepped up to get the Scots out of trouble when, three plays later, Herman Carroll tipped a Pelluer pass which was picked off by safety George Coghill, who ran it back 32 yards for a touchdown.

Hastings was on the money with the extra point and the Claymores were back in the driving-seat at 17–10. But Matthews made his fourth error of the day when he was again intercepted by Dixon at the start of the fourth quarter, although the Germans couldn't capitalise when Kleinmann missed his field goal attempt from 44 yards. Brad Bretz replaced the out-of-sorts Pelluer but saw his first endzone pass intercepted, again by George Coghill, as Galaxy tried to battle back. The Germans were rewarded on their next possession though, when Bretz fired a pass to dangerman Jay

Kearney, who ran 44 yards down the sideline to make the catch for the game-tying score at the two-minute warning.

It looked as if the game was headed for overtime, but coach Criner decided to go for the jugular with just under a minute remaining. Switching to his two-minute offence Matthews hit LaChapelle for 21- and 28-yard gains, the receiver running patterns that would take him out of bounds to control the clock, and the Claymores into field goal range. With just six seconds on the clock, and the thought of those two earlier misses still fresh in his mind, McCallum had a chance to redeem himself and win the day for the Claymores. A nerve-jangling 46-yard kick was the test, but the Canadian-Scot kept his cool and made a confident strike to send the ball soaring through the uprights, laying the ghost of Arden Czyzeweski to rest.

The little kicker almost ran the length of the field before being swamped by his team-mates in celebration as the 13,116 roared its approval. The Claymores had completed the double over reigning champions Galaxy to extend their lead at the top of the World League to 6–1. Afterwards McCallum admitted: 'It's been a tough two weeks and I just haven't been hitting the ball well. I was under pressure after my first two misses but I just kept my

GAME STATISTICS

WEEK 7: FRANKFURT GALAXY at SCOTTISH CLAYMORES; MURRAYFIELD, EDINBURGH; 26 MAY 1996; ATT: 13,116; WEATHER: CLOUDY, 12°C

SCORE BY PERIODS

	1	2	3	4	
GALAXY	7	0	3	7	17
CLAYMORES	0	3	14	3	20

SCORING SUMMARY

Team	Period	Elapsed Time	Play	Score
Fra	1st	10:09	TD, Hall 27 interception (Kleinmann PAT)	7-0
Sco	2nd	4:16	FG, McCallum 28	7-3
Sco	3rd	4:33	TD, LaChapelle 52 pass Matthews (Hastings PAT)	7-10
Fra	3rd	8:56	FG, Kleinmann 32	10-10
Sco	3rd	13:07	TD, Coghill 32 interception (Hastings PAT)	10-17
Fra	4th	14:03	TD, Kearney 44 pass Bretz (Kleinmann PAT)	17-17
Sco	4th	14:49	FG, McCallum 46	17-20

TEAM STATISTICS

	GALAXY	CLAYMORES
First Downs	20	17
Rushes/Yards	19/57	33/108
Net Passing Yards	271	251
Total Net Yards	328	359
Passing (A-C-I)	44/22/3	25/14/4
Punts/Average	5/43.2	3/31.6
Fumbles/Lost	1/0	2/2
Penalties	5/40	5/35
Time of Possession	29:55	30:05

INDIVIDUAL STATISTICS

RUSHING

Galaxy: Bender 2-7; Seibert 13-36; Williams 1-0; Pelluer 1-9; Bolton 1-5; Harrell 1-0

Claymores: Stacy 25-102; Dickerson 3-4; Kaaiohelo 3-1; Matthews 3-1

PASSING

Galaxy: Pelluer 30-15-151, 0TD, 2INT; Bretz 14-7-143, 1TD, 1INT

Claymores: Matthews 25-14-267, 1TD, 4INT

RECEIVING

Galaxy: Bellamy 5-64; Seibert 3-17; Harrell 2-32; Kearney 7-126-1; Bailey 3-32; Bender 1-16; Harrison 1-7

Claymores: Couper 3-45; LaChapelle 7-182-1; Dickerson 1-30; Tate 1-8; Stacy 2-2 head down on the last kick and concentrated on making a good swing. Fortunately it went through.'

A relieved coach Criner said: 'Even though Paul missed two kicks he got the one that counted, and I've forgiven him already.' And he added: 'I've always said that championships are won on the back of good defence and that was proved today. Our defence performed like real champions. They kept coming up with the big plays and gave us the opportunity to win the game.'

PAUL McCALLUM: CANADIAN COOL

By the time Paul McCallum arrived at the Scottish Claymores, he had already sampled both sides of the sporting coin. Trial stints with St Mirren and Hamilton Accies failed to land him a contract back in 1990, ensuring he would not follow in the footsteps of cousin Brian O'Neil, currently carving out a successful soccer career with Celtic.

But on his return to Vancouver, McCallum took the decision which would guarantee him a place in the annals of Scottish sporting history. On the invitation of a friend, McCallum tried out as a kicker for Canadian Football League team the British Columbia Lions. His prowess was immediately evident. Subsequent spells with the Ottawa Rough Riders and current club Saskatchewan Roughriders merely reinforced the fact that McCallum had what it takes to succeed at the highest level in football.

But there was one more formidable hurdle to overcome before he could claim his place in the Claymores' line-up: the legendary Gavin Hastings. McCallum, who had been rejected by former Claymores head coach Lary Kuharich back in 1995, admits he approached the 1996 training camp ready to go to war in a bid to claim his place. 'Basically, I was being regarded as an also-ran by a lot of people,' he said. 'Everyone assumed that Gavin would make the transition from kicking a rugby ball to kicking a football without any great difficulty. That meant I had to be totally single-minded in my approach to training camp because I simply had to get everything right.

'Don't get me wrong, I was prepared to help Gavin in any way I could because he wasn't foolish enough to think he'd just turn up and bang the ball through the

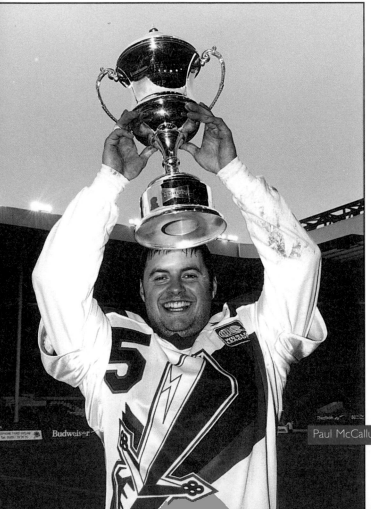

Paul McCallum shows off the Budweiser Cup

uprights. I knew he was as desperate as I was to make the squad, but I wasn't going to walk away if he asked for my help. We became good friends, but there was also tremendous rivalry between us because to all intents and purposes we were two men competing for the same job.'

In the end, Jim Criner solved the problem by selecting both men in his squad. McCallum was handed the responsibility of kicking field goals and punting while Hastings handled points after kick-off. Criner's choice proved to be inspired as the steely McCallum came through for the Claymores when it mattered, despite a mid-season form slump.

His nerve was never in question after a 27-yard field goal in overtime against the London Monarchs gave the Claymores a winning start to the season and clinched the Budweiser Cup. But a 47-yard, last-second field goal against Frankfurt at Murrayfield left even the most cynical Claymores fans with a lump in their throats as the likeable McCallum took off in celebration like a demented aeroplane. 'I've made longer kicks to win games,' he said, 'but that had to be one of the most vital.

'I was going through a sticky spell with my kicking and missing field goals I would expect to nail. I wasn't able to work out why and that was the most frustrating part. Gavin was a great help to me then because he kept my confidence up and kept urging me to relax while we were on the sidelines. In the end I sussed out the problem myself. I had been trying to hit the ball too hard and once I got my rhythm back and concentrated on getting a smooth contact with the ball it was sailing true again.'

McCallum's end-of-season form was truly stunning. He became the first man in World League history to nail two four-point field goals in a season. A 51-yard effort against London at Murrayfield was followed by a 50-yard kick in the World Bowl against Frankfurt as McCallum made himself a hero to team-mates and fans alike. Typically, the modest McCallum shrugs off that hero status. 'I was just doing what I was paid to do,' he said. 'If you miss a field goal, you're the villain. If you put the important kicks through, you're the hero. It goes with the territory, and if you start getting big-headed about a little bit of success, you'll soon find success is short-lived. Sure as hell, the moment you start thinking there's not much to this game, it will bite right back at you.'

That down-to-earth approach wavered just once during the season. McCallum's pride in his dual nationality prompted him to head off to a Glasgow tattoo artist to have the Canadian and Scottish flags etched on his left leg prior to the World Bowl. But the 26-year-old admits it was one of the few times in the season when things didn't go quite as he planned them.

'I went to a guy Scott Couper recommended,' he said, 'because Scott has a tattoo of Michael Jordan on his shoulder. I drew out the design I wanted and my original plan was to have an American football under the Canadian flag and a soccer ball under the Scottish flag. But the whole damned process was so painful I wound up telling the guy to stop when the flags were completed. Maybe I'll summon up the courage at some point in the future to have the job completed.'

WEEK 8: SUNK BY THE ADMIRALS

Scottish Claymores 27 at Amsterdam Admirals 31

Winning the right to host the World Bowl at Murrayfield was one thing, but keeping the intensity up to take that winning momentum into the final was proving a tough task for the Claymores as they travelled to Amsterdam to face the Admirals, who had never lost at home during the regular season in the Olympish Stadion. 'It has been a constant battle to keep the intensity up,' admitted Jim Criner. 'We've found it's been increasingly difficult to keep the players' focus on each of the upcoming games. It is hard to keep your edge when all the other teams are fighting like dogs to play you in the final.'

One player who was focused for the week eight rematch was former Claymores defensive tackle Troy Ridgley, cut by Criner four weeks earlier to solve a numbers problem but picked up the following week by the Admirals. Ridgley was looking forward to coming face to face with his old team-mates. 'I'm a little more fired up than normal simply because I'd like the Claymores coaching staff to feel by the end of the game that they made a mistake when they cut me.'

Mistakes were in evidence during an error-filled first

GAME STATISTICS

WEEK 8: SCOTTISH CLAYMORES at AMSTERDAM ADMIRALS; OLYMPISH STADION, AMSTERDAM; 1 JUNE 1996; ATT: 10,501; WEATHER SUNNY, 12°C

SCORE BY PERIODS

	1	2	3	4	
CLAYMORES	0	0	21	6	27
ADMIRALS	0	10	7	14	31

SCORING SUMMARY

Team	Period	Elapsed Time	Play	Score
Ams	2nd	1:30	FG, Vinateri 18	0-3
Ams	2nd	5:19	TD, Chandler 7 pass Furrer (Vinatieri PAT)	0-10
Sco	3rd	3:33	TD, LaChapelle 14 pass Ballard (Hastings PAT)	7-10
Sco	3rd	7:27	TD, Gissendaner 21 reverse (Hastings PAT)	14-10
Sco	3rd	9:23	TD, Murphy 7 pass Ballard (Hastings PAT)	21-10
Ams	3rd	14:03	TD, Bobo 14 pass Furrer (Vinatieri PAT)	21-17
Sco	4th	4:15	TD, LaChapelle 33 pass Ballard (PAT blocked)	27-17
Ams	4th	7:28	TD, Bobo 14 pass Furrer (Vinatieri PAT)	27-24
Ams	4th	11:17	TD, Furrer 46 scramble (Vinatieri PAT)	27-31

TEAM STATISTICS

	CLAYMORES	ADMIRALS
First Downs	14	21
Rushes/Yards	19/62	22/130
Net Passing Yards	230	268
Total Net Yards	292	398
Passing (A-C-I)	32/15/1	43/23/0
Punts/Average	7/37.7	5/39.8
Fumbles/Lost	0/0	1/1
Penalties	7/62	7/63
Time of Possession	26:51	33:03

INDIVIDUAL STATISTICS

RUSHING
Claymores: Stacy 10-4; Matthews 2-13; Gissendaner 1-21-1; Kaaiohelo 2-11; Thomas 1-2; Ballard 2-5; Dickerson 1-2
Admirals: Wright 9-33; Furrer 4-84-1; Bryant 5-18; Sacca 4-(-5)

PASSING
Claymores: Matthews 16-4-52, 0TD, 0INT; Ballard 16-11-189, 3TD, 1INT
Admirals: Furrer 43-23-289, 3TD, 0INT

RECEIVING
Claymores: LaChapelle 7-159-12; Dickerson 2-13; Murphy 1-7-1; Stacy 1-4
Admirals: Bryant 1-1; Bobo 7-123-2; Chandler 6-79-1; Wright 1-1; Etheridge 1-8; Smith 3-19

A Claymores and Admirals pile-up

'HOW 'BOUT THEM CLAYMORES!'

Jared Kaaiohelo makes his move

quarter and neither team looked like scoring until Adam Vinatieri put the Dutch on the scoreboard with an 18-yard field goal at the start of the second quarter. Admirals passer Will Furrer, untroubled by a non-existent Claymores pass rush, found receiver Darren Chandler wide open in the endzone with a six-yard touchdown pass to make it 10–0. The Claymores couldn't reply and finished the half with a dismal 66 yards total offence, World League leading rusher Siran Stacy limited to only 14 yards. It went from bad to worse at the start of the second half when Steve Matthews went down injured with bruised ribs after what appeared to be a late hit from Admirals defensive tackle Jim Hanna.

But the incident proved a turning point for the Claymores when back-up Jim Ballard replaced Matthews and quickly got to work, firing a precise 23-yard pass to Sean LaChapelle. Three plays later, LaChapelle was in the endzone after catching another Ballard pass to go 14-yards down the sideline and into the endzone for the Claymores' first score. Hastings kicked the PAT and the Claymores were back in contention at 10–7. Defensive end Ty Parten then forced the Admirals to punt, batting down a Furrer pass before Ballard picked up where he left off and aired out a deep sideline throw to LaChapelle to chalk up a 63-yard gain.

Criner then called a reverse play, Stacy handing off to receiver Lee Gissendaner who ran in for a 21-yard score. Hastings was good again with the extra point and the Claymores were in front at 14–10. The Claymores defence made another big play on Amsterdam's next possession to silence the 10,501 Dutch crowd. End John DeWitt swatted the ball from Furrer's grasp, recovering it himself at the Admirals' two-yard line. Ballard took advantage of DeWitt's enterprise two plays later lobbing a beautifully timed seven-yard pass to receiver Yo Murphy, who executed a perfect fade pattern to catch the ball in the endzone. Hastings's third successful PAT moved the Scots into a 21–10 lead as Admirals head coach Al Luginbill threw a tantrum on the sideline. Luginbill's theatrics must have helped motivate his team though, with Furrer throwing a 40-yard touchdown pass to receiver Phillip Bobo, to make it 21–17 at the end of the third quarter.

Ballard hit back for the Scots at the start of the fourth, firing another stunning pass to LaChapelle and the receiver sliced through the Admirals' coverage on a corner route for a 33-yard touchdown score. However, Hastings's extra point was blocked and the Claymores had to settle for a 10-point lead at 27–17. With plenty of time on the clock Furrer calmly directed his team downfield on a six-play, 65-yard drive, capped with a 14-yard touchdown pass to Bobo, who flew past Claymores cornerback James Williams for the score. Vinatieri's conversion meant the Admirals were now only three points behind at 24–27.

The Scots were forced to punt on their next possession, and two plays later Will Furrer caught the Claymores defence napping by running a quarterback draw, magnificently scrambling 46 yards down the sideline to break the Bravehearts. The Claymores had a chance to mount a comeback but Ballard ruined an almost perfect passing day, picked off decisively by Admirals safety Robert O'Neal as he attempted to move the Scots downfield with a pass to LaChapelle. 'I was happy with the way that I played, apart from that last throw,' said Ballard, who had waited eight games to play. 'But I have to learn from my mistakes and hopefully we can get back on track next week against my old team London.'

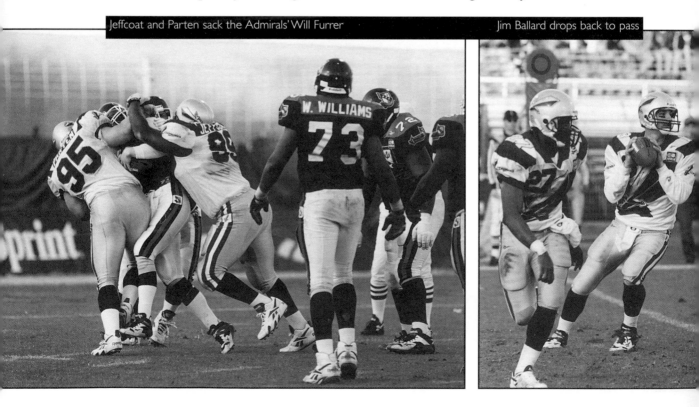

Jeffcoat and Parten sack the Admirals' Will Furrer

Jim Ballard drops back to pass

A GOOD YEAR FOR THE NATIONALS

Since the inception of the World League everyone has had a view on the role of home-based 'national' players on each of the six European teams. Should inexperienced players be allowed to play alongside seasoned veterans taking part in the high-speed, high-impact and at times downright dangerous world of professional gridiron? Then there's the theory that suggests it's vital to involve home-grown talent to develop the game in the host countries, and although coming from the amateur to the professional game has its risks, given time and good coaching, national players will develop to become integral parts of any pro squad.

If the experiences of this season of the seven Claymores national players is anything to go by, then it's the latter argument which has been proved true in Scotland. Scott Couper, Ben Torriero, Gavin Hastings, Paul McCallum, Robert Flickinger, Emmett Waldron and J.P. Nummi were all names that became as familiar as any star of the World League to Claymores fans this year. That these players had become notables playing under the World League's national ruling that allows 50 per cent of game time to be afforded in the inclusion of a European player on both sides of the ball, is a testament to how these true stars of the World League shone.

All with the exception of Nummi, who had been grouped with a defensive back unit that a player of Ronnie Lott's calibre would have found it difficult getting a starting spot on, had substantial amounts of game time, partly due to the adaptation of the National Rule but more down to the fact that each proved himself as an athlete capable of competing at the top level.

The statistics this season proved the argument. To start with, in the receiving department, Couper boasted numbers to rival any World League wide out. In the course of the ten-week

regular season he amassed 12 catches for 165 yards, averaging 13.8 yards per catch, his longest being a 36-yard touchdown catch against Barcelona in the final week of the season. He added that to his first glorious and unforgettable touchdown which helped the Claymores defeat Amsterdam in week three, earning World League National-Player-of-the-Week honours after his performance.

The Glasgow Lions stand-out laid all the credit for his success in the excellent coaching he received this season but also in the adoption of the National Rule. 'Last year I was just happy to be watching, sitting on the sideline and getting in for the occasional play. I never expected to get a lot of game time and that was fine,' said Couper. 'But this year, with the National Rule, I knew I had to step it up and improve my game because I knew I would be playing.

'I think adopting the rule has been a total success. You just had to take a look around the league to see how the nationals had contributed from week one. After Sammi Alalampi's World League record 87-yard touchdown it was

Gavin Hastings sings *Flower of Scotland*

'HOW 'BOUT THEM CLAYMORES!'

just a total success story and I think we've reached a position where a national scored on every team. I think involving nationals did a lot to involve the fans and will also help at the grass-roots level. If kids see that it is possible to play, they will want to become footballers and that, in the long run, can only be a good thing for the game here in Europe.'

Couper is putting his time where his mouth is and, following last year's success of the Claymores kids' coaching clinics, he has joined forces with national coach Mike Kenny in setting up a Flag Football league in Scotland during the off-season. But away from his community contribution the 26-year-old receiver took a lot out of the Claymores' championship season. 'For me personally, the National Rule made me look at the game in a different way, knowing that I had to perform and had a role to play. In that respect this last season has been a bit of a growing-up process for me.

'I suppose, with the increased playing time, you could say that I'm beginning to mature as a footballer, although I've still a long way to go. Playing with receivers like Sean LaChapelle and Yo Murphy also helped. Their talent is phenomenal and fortunately for me it seems to have rubbed off a little, and along with the superb coaching I've been getting from coaches Criner, Sochor and Alcalde, I feel my improvement has been immense. I feel this season that I earned the confidence of my coaches and that made me feel a valued member of the team.'

Torriero, voted a special teams captain by his team-mates at the start of the season, was one of the team's leading players on that unit, accruing three unassisted tackles – bettered only by James Fuller and Frank Robinson – as well as two bruising kick-off returns for a total of 21

yards. Flickinger, too, made his mark on special teams – winning a National-Player-of-the-Week award for his role in the Claymores' win over Frankfurt at Murrayfield – with two open-field tackles. Until he was injured in week eight, Flick also made his presence felt on the defensive line – a remarkable achievement after converting, under the guidance of line coach Bill Dutton, from the tight end position he played at the Monarchs.

Perhaps the biggest success, though, was achieved by Waldron, a player with college experience at Rice University, who was a key member of the Claymores' defence. Waldron earned enough of his coaches' confidence to be placed in a regular rotation with defensive captain and fellow middle-linebacker Mark Sander, where he made 25 unassisted tackles and forced a fumble, not to mention three tackles on kick-off duty.

But the biggest contribution in terms of points scored came from the two national kickers, Hastings and McCallum, epitomised by McCallum's 46-yard game-winning field goal against Frankfurt, his match-winner against London in week one and his 51-yard four pointer in the return against the Auld Enemy at Murrayfield. Hastings was a model of consistency from the 19-yard line on extra points and rifled through 23 of 27 PAT attempts, while maintaining a solid performance on kick-offs. McCallum finished the season third in the league in kicking, notching up 34 points from 11 field goals out of 15 attempts, his longest the pressure kick that downed Galaxy.

All in all, it was a good year for the nationals.

WEEK 9: THE MONARCHS ARE CROWNED
London Monarchs 28 at Scottish Claymores 33

All five remaining teams had a chance to make it to the World Bowl with only two weeks of the regular season left, although the Claymores' week-nine opponents, London Monarchs, were an outside bet. The Monarchs had to win all of their remaining games to have any chance after being dealt the dual blow of going down 7–6 to Barcelona Dragons and also losing star attraction William 'The Refrigerator' Perry, who had returned to the US for treatment to a knee injury.

The Claymores were also having to pick themselves up following the defeat in Amsterdam and the loss of No.1 draft pick Ty Parten, who would miss the remainder of the season with a knee ligament injury. However, Jim Criner didn't need to expend too much effort in rekindling his team's intensity to face the Auld Enemy at Murrayfield. Pre-match ticket sales had gone well and translated into 15,461 – the biggest crowd of the season so far – turning out for the derby game. The Claymores had relied on their hard-hitting defence to carry the day in previous victories, but after Jim Ballard's second-half display in Amsterdam, in which the quarterback had thrown an impressive three touchdowns and 189 yards from only 11 passes, hopes were high for an offensive revival as the quarterback made his first start.

But the Monarchs were to spoil the Murrayfield party, getting on the scoreboard first, when quarterback Preston Jones fired a four-yard touchdown pass to New Zealand receiver Willie Hinchcliff. National player Kevin Hurst's extra point made it 7–0 to the Monarchs, but his kick was to be eclipsed by Paul McCallum who booted through a massive 51-yard field goal – the longest in the Claymores' history – for four points. That huge conversion seemed to lift the Scots and Ballard kept the momentum going at the start of the second quarter completing a simple flare pass to Ron Dickerson at London's 35-yard line. Dickerson showed a remarkable turn of pace, though, powering down the sideline past tacklers before diving into the endzone to convert the short gain play into a stunning touchdown score.

With the Claymores 10-7 ahead London attempted to get back into the game, but Jones was intercepted by Claymores defensive end John DeWitt. However, Scotland failed to capitalise when Gavin Hastings, having an off day, missed out on converting his first ever field goal, wide right from 24 yards. Hastings made amends, booting through an extra point at the end of the first half after receiver Yo Murphy scooped in a 12-yard pass from Ballard.

Trailing 17–7, the Monarchs pulled the deficit back to three points at the start of the third quarter when cornerback Darren Studstill intercepted Ballard deep in Claymores territory. Receiver Larry Wallace then caught a 10-yard lob from Jones for another London score, as the game developed into a shoot-out. McCallum added a 30-yard

GAME STATISTICS

WEEK 9: LONDON MONARCHS at SCOTTISH CLAYMORES; MURRAYFIELD, EDINBURGH; 9 JUNE 1996; ATT: 15,461; WEATHER: SUNNY, 13°C

SCORE BY PERIODS

	1	2	3	4	
MONARCHS	7	0	7	14	28
CLAYMORES	4	13	0	16	33

SCORING SUMMARY

Team	Period	Elapsed Time	Play	Score
Lon	1st	3:37	TD, Hinchcliff 4 pass Jones (Hurst PAT)	7-0
Sco	1st	11:38	FG, McCallum 51	7-4
Sco	2nd	4:07	TD, Dickerson 35 pass Ballard	7-10
Sco	2nd	14:23	TD, Murphy 12 pass Ballard (Hastings PAT)	7-17
Lon	3rd	8:54	TD, Wallace 10 pass Jones (Hurst PAT)	14-17
Sco	4th	0:51	FG, McCallum 30	14-20
Sco	4th	9:22	TD, Murphy 15 pass Ballard (Hastings PAT)	14-27
Lon	4th	11:35	TD, Wallace 19 pass Jones (Hurst PAT)	21-27
Sco	4th	13:23	TD, Stacy 43 run	21-33
Lon	4th	14:47	TD, Titley 2 pass Jones (Hurst PAT)	28-33

TEAM STATISTICS

	MONARCHS	CLAYMORES
First Downs	23	19
Rushes/Yards	12/78	29/134
Net Passing Yards	314	236
Total Net Yards	392	370
Passing (A-C-I)	46/28/2	24/17/1
Punts/Average	6/46.2	2/38.5
Fumbles/Lost	1/0	1/1
Penalties	9/60	5/45
Time of Possession	27:54	32:06

INDIVIDUAL STATISTICS

RUSHING
Monarchs: Vinson 8-43; Green 3-4; White 1-31
Claymores: Stacy 19-100-1; Dickerson 3-6; Kaaiohelo 1-3

PASSING
Monarchs: Jones 45-28-335, 4TD, 2INT; Green 1-0-0
Claymores: Ballard 24-17-243, 3TD, 1INT

RECEIVING
Monarchs: Green 1-5; Hinchcliff 3-18-1; Titley 8-117-1; Howard 4-55; White 5-44; Wallace 5-80-2; Vinson 2-16
Claymores: Dickerson 4-70-1; Stacy 3-6; LaChapelle 2-50; Murphy 3-29-2; Tate 3-49; Couper 1-30; Kaaiohelo 1-9

Tom Barndt blocks for Siran Stacy

Jim Ballard looks for his receiver

field goal at the start of the fourth quarter to make it 20–14 and ten plays later the Claymores were in the endzone again, Ballard completing his second touchdown pass to Yo Murphy, this time from 15-yards, the little receiver proving Sean LaChapelle was not the only receiving threat on the Scots' squad.

Hastings's extra point moved the Claymores into a 27–14 lead with six minutes to go. But London, trying to keep their faint World Bowl hopes alive, were not dead and with three minutes remaining Jones passed to Wallace again, who broke two Claymores tackles to dive into the endzone for the score. Hurst's PAT made it 27–21 and the Scots still had work to do. Fittingly, it was the Claymores' workhorse, running back Siran Stacy, who was to tip the balance. The productive rusher had already notched up 100 yards on the day and had passed another World League benchmark in the third quarter, going over the 2,000-yards barrier in all-purpose yards gained.

Stacy took control now and drove the Claymores from their 20-yard line into Monarchs territory before powering through tackles at the line of scrimmage to run 43 yards into the endzone for the game's decisive score. 'Teams are coming out to shut our running game down and at times it gets frustrating,' said Stacy afterwards. 'But I've got the offensive line to pick me up and if I can get the ball

20–25 times a game I'm going to make some big plays. I don't care what kind of defence they play.'

The Monarchs got a consolation touchdown when tight end Mike Titley caught a two-yard pass from Jones for a touchdown, but with only eight seconds remaining it was too little, too late. Gavin Hastings's tackle on the Monarchs' desperate on-side kick ended the game, the Claymores victorious at 33–28.

The Scots were back on track with the offence firing under Ballard's direction. The quarterback had thrown 17 passes for 243 yards and three touchdowns, for the second week running, to post the Claymores' biggest ever scoring spree. 'I waited all year to get my chance and this week I got an opportunity to show what I could do,' said Ballard. 'When you get an opportunity you've got to make the most of it and thankfully that's what's happened.'

'Our team did a great job today,' said Jim Criner. 'We knew it was going to be tough, and it was. But we came out and performed as a team, and despite the fact that we sustained a few injuries, I feel confident things are back on track for the World Bowl.'

Siran Stacy summed up the mood, saying: 'Once again it feels good to kick some English butt!'

SIRAN STACY: RUSHING TO GLORY

The persistence of Jim Criner and Claymores general manager Mike Keller in persuading

Siran Stacy to throw in his lot with the team again proved to be the crucial factor in the success story of 1996. Stacy admits he'd had a gutful of the Claymores and the World League after the disastrous campaign of 1995. The running back from Geneva, Alabama, was one of the few successes of that first season as he racked up 785 yards on 214 carries. But when Criner called him and asked if he would work his magic again the answer was a resounding 'No!'. The decision by every NFL team to ignore his efforts for the Claymores had left the 27-year-old a disillusioned man.

But anyone who knows Mike Keller knows he'll never take no for an answer, and by the time the Claymores convened in Atlanta, his powers of persuasion ensured Stacy

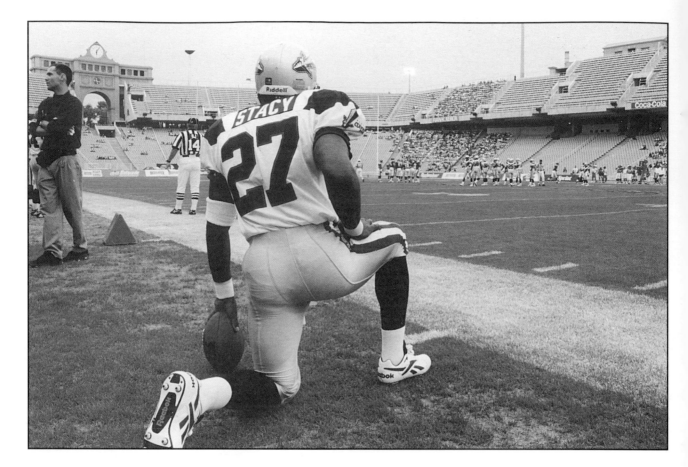

was suited up and ready to play. The rest is history. Stacy became the first player in World League history to record two 500-yard rushing seasons. He became the leading rusher in World League history with 1,565 yards and his nine touchdowns in the season helped take his career rushing tally to 12, another World League record.

Not surprisingly, Stacy has no regrets about the change of heart which brought him back to Scotland. 'Being rejected by the NFL hurt me a lot and I had pretty much decided to call it a day as far as football was concerned,' he said. 'The way things panned out with the team last season made it less than enjoyable to be involved in. I had made my mind up I didn't want to be a part of that again. Coach Criner and Mike Keller assured me things would be different but I really wasn't sure about coming back.

'I was so depressed and disillusioned when the NFL rejected me that it took months before I started putting my life back in order. Once I had taken the decision to go back to school and finish my degree in Criminal Justice, it was a real eye-opener for me. I was sampling life outside of football and discovering just how enjoyable it was. So when football came along again, I wasn't sure I wanted it maybe ruining my life again. In the end I took the gamble and I'm so glad I did.'

At just 5ft 10in, Stacy is a pigmy in a game played by giants. Those giants dish out punishment aplenty as they zero in on the running back each time he carries the ball. The

Stacy doing what he does best

bruising effects of a long, hard season take their toll on Stacy's body, but he wouldn't have it any other way. He knows that every time he winds up at the bottom of the pile of bodies, he's racked up vital yards or claimed another touchdown. 'You don't feel the pain of being hit at the time because the adrenalin is really pumping during a game,' he said. 'But when you pick yourself up and see they've sent their best men to try and stop you it gives you a real buzz.

'As soon as you get back to the huddle you're hoping your number is called for the next play and you get another chance to carry the ball. Let's face it, that's what you're out there for in the first place. When you wake up the following morning you think, "Man, I ache all over". But the feeling of satisfaction if the team has won and you've contributed makes every aching muscle worth while. There is no greater feeling than that.'

The vastly experienced Stacy played all 16 regular season games for the Philadelphia Eagles back in 1992. And that experience has taught him that while records may be nice to hold, nothing compares to winning. 'People talk about this record I've set and that record I've set, but I pay very little attention to stats,' he said. 'Put it this way: if I make 200 yards in a game and the Claymores lose, it has all been for nothing. I'd far rather make 50 yards if the Claymores come out on top at the end of the day. Of course, in an ideal world I'd make 200 yards every week and the Claymores would also win every week.'

Unlike so many in sport, Stacy never forgets the unsung heroes who put their bodies on the line to make him one of the stars of the team. 'This game is not about one man; there are 11 guys working their tails off out there,' he said. 'I wouldn't get a single yard if there weren't people blocking for me. Guys like Ron Dickerson, Jared Kaaiohelo and Markus Thomas were throwing lead blocks for me week in, week out. The same was true of the offensive line. If you can't make yards running behind guys like Purvis Hunt and Keith Wagner, you'll never make them.

'That was the beauty of the 1996 Claymores. We worked as a team and there were no bigheads or superstar mentalities. It was a real pleasure to play alongside these guys and I thank God I took the chance to come back over. Giving the Scottish fans the World Bowl was just the icing on the cake. I really felt I owed them something for the superb way they had treated me and I just hope the World Bowl helps settle my debt.'

WEEK 10: SLAIN BY THE DRAGONS
Scottish Claymores 27 at Barcelona Dragons 32

With Amsterdam and Frankfurt contesting what amounted to a World Bowl decider, the Claymores could have been forgiven for letting their minds drift away from the meaningless final regular season match with Barcelona at the Montjuic Stadium. However, Jim Criner

Gavin Hastings kicks off

didn't see it that way. 'I'm not thinking about who we will be playing in the World Bowl,' said the coach. 'In fact, we won't even look at the result of that game until Monday, *after* we've taken care of our own business down in Barcelona.'

With the Bowl game only a week away, Criner did make one concession and stood down a number of his starters, although the Scots would be without receiver/returner Lee Gissendaner and national Robert Flickinger, both ruled out with respective shoulder and elbow injuries. Criner bulked up his squad signing NFL veteran lineman Jason Buck and former Admirals receiver Derek Hill. But the coach warned: 'We'll be playing against a team who have fallen on hard times, have nothing to lose and have the best-rated defence in the league. We expect to have our hands full.'

Indeed, the World-Bowl bound Claymores had their hands full from the start, running back Charles Thompson powering the Dragons down-field on their second possession before quarterback Kelly Holcomb dived over on a one-yard sneak to open the scoring. The Claymores got back into the game at the start of the second quarter when Jim Ballard unleashed a 72-yard pass to Sean LaChapelle. The Kansas City Chiefs allocated receiver's huge gain was turned

GAME STATISTICS

WEEK 10: SCOTTISH CLAYMORES at BARCELONA DRAGONS; MONTJUIC STADIUM, BARCELONA; 16 JUNE 1996; ATT: 16,124; WEATHER: SUNNY, 20°C

SCORE BY PERIODS

	1	2	3	4	
CLAYMORES	0	7	6	14	27
DRAGONS	7	7	9	9	32

SCORING SUMMARY

Team	Period	Elapsed Time	Play	Score
Bar	1st	10:29	TD, Holcomb 1 run (Szeredy PAT)	0-7
Sco	2nd	1:35	TD, Stacy 2 run (Hastings PAT)	7-7
Bar	2nd	5:54	TD, Wilburn 16 run (Szeredy PAT)	7-14
Sco	3rd	3:08	TD, Couper 36 pass Ballard (PAT missed)	13-14
Bar	3rd	7:43	Ballard sacked Heinrich endzone safety	13-16
Bar	3rd	11:38	TD, Browning 51 pass Holcomb (Szeredy PAT)	13-23
Sco	4th	2:22	TD, Stacy 5 run (Hastings PAT)	20-23
Bar	4th	4:38	FG, Szeredy 33	20-26
Sco	4th	11:23	TD, Murphy 17 pass Ballard (Hastings PAT)	27-26
Bar	4th	14:28	TD, Sacca 1 run	27-32

TEAM STATISTICS

	CLAYMORES	DRAGONS
First Downs	23	22
Rushes/Yards	27/91	30/132
Net Passing Yards	309	252
Total Net Yards	400	384
Passing (A-C-I)	27/22/0	25/15/0
Punts/Average	4/39	4/40
Fumbles/Lost	0/0	5/1
Penalties	5/50	7/40
Time of Possession	31:30	28:30

INDIVIDUAL STATISTICS

RUSHING
Claymores: Stacy 19-76-2; Ballard 4-15; Dickerson 3-(-3); Kaaiohelo 1-0
Dragons: Wilburn 12-68-1; Thompson 11-44; Holcomb 5-29-1; Sacca 1-1-1

PASSING
Claymores: Ballard 27-22-355, 2TD, 0INT
Dragons: Holcomb 20-11-202, 1TD, 0INT; Sacca 5-4-81, 0TD, 0INT

RECEIVING
Claymores: Murphy 5-104-1; Stacy 3-82; Dickerson 3-30; LaChapelle 2-83; Couper 2-46-1; Tate 1-5; Hill 1-5
Dragons: Browning 5-131-1; Davis 3-19; Burkett 2-40; Burnett 2-10; Shedd 1-64; Alalampi 1-13; Wilburn 1-6

FINAL STANDINGS

	W	L	T	%	PF	PA
Scottish Claymores*	7	3	0	.700	233	190
Frankfurt Galaxy†	6	4	0	.600	221	220
Amsterdam Admirals	5	5	0	.500	250	210
Barcelona Dragons	5	5	0	.500	192	230
London Monarchs	4	6	0	.400	161	192
Rhein Fire	3	7	0	.300	176	191

* Qualified for World Bowl 96 as first-half champions on head-to-head tie-breaker against Frankfurt
† Qualified for World Bowl 96 on overall record

into points on the next play when Siran Stacy powered over from two yards for the touchdown. But the home team, in front of 16,124 supporters, were proving difficult opponents and rusher Terry Wilburn showed up a lack of concentration in the Scots' defence, breaking tackles *en route* to a 16-yard touchdown run to give the Dragons a 14–7 half-time lead. Claymores defensive co-ordinator Ray Willsey was furious with his unit's slack tackling and emphasised his dissatisfaction during the break.

The Scots were given a shot in the arm on their first possession of the second half when Ballard fired a 36-yard pass to Glaswegian receiver Scott Couper. The Strathclyde University PhD student showed skill that would not be out of place in the NFL diving into the endzone, between two defenders, to record his second pro touchdown. But Gavin Hastings missed the extra point and, on the Claymores' next series, Ballard was sacked in his own endzone by Dragons lineman Josh Heinrich for a two-point safety and a 16–13 lead. The Dragons advanced that lead at the end of the third quarter when Holcomb threw up a bomb and receiver Alphonzo Browning came down with a 51-yard touchdown catch to make it 23–13.

Scotland fought back, mounting a 12-play drive at the start of the fourth quarter, capped by a five-yard charge into the endzone by Stacy. The Dragons reasserted their authority, though, when Scott Szeredy kicked a 33-yard field goal to post a 26–20 lead. The shoot-out continued as the Claymores took back the initiative when Ballard lobbed a screen pass to Yo Murphy, who darted around behind his blockers before stretching into the endzone to tie the game. Gavin Hastings's PAT gave the Claymores a one-point lead but with three minutes remaining, the Dragons took over.

Replacing Holcomb with Tony Sacca, Barcelona coach Jack Bicknell called in his two-minute offence, and the Dragons moved into scoring range. The Claymores' tired defence couldn't respond to the attack and with 32 seconds on the clock Sacca dived into the endzone on a one-yard quarterback sneak to hand victory to the Dragons. The Claymores would now have to pick themselves up to face the threat of a resurgent Frankfurt Galaxy after the reigning World Bowl champions had come out on top by 28–20 in a thrilling victory over Amsterdam.

'We were hoping for some winning momentum going into next week's game but it wasn't to be,' said a disappointed Jim Ballard. 'We've beaten Frankfurt twice already but that doesn't mean anything in the World Bowl. We now have a job to do in preparing for the big one.' And Jim Criner added: 'We're now going to have to rally for the World Bowl. Frankfurt are a very good football team and we're going to have to play much better if we are going to win our first championship.'

JIM BALLARD: THE PATIENT PASSER

If ever a guy deserved a break it was Jim Ballard. When he finally got it, the feel-good factor extended to every single fan of the Scottish Claymores. Ballard started his World League career with the London Monarchs after being allocated from the Cincinatti Bengals back in 1995. The Bengals cut him midway through the World League season and bad was followed by worse as the Monarchs dumped him almost immediately. The Claymores stepped in to offer him a place in the league's worst team and, to his credit, Ballard jumped at the chance.

So began a love affair with Scotland which saw him return again this year, only to find himself taking his place in the queue for a starting slot in the line-up. As late as four days before the season opener in London, Jim Criner was still touting Ballard as his starting quarterback for the season. But the 24-year-old found himself on the outside looking in again as a late form surge by Kansas City Chiefs allocated player Steve Matthews proved sufficient to earn him the nod.

Ballard's frustration would continue for seven weeks before an injury to Matthews gave him his chance in the second half of the match in Amsterdam. To say he grabbed his opportunity with both hands would be the understatement of the year. An offence which had been struggling to put points on the board was suddenly on fire with the native of Akron, Ohio, calling the shots. They racked up 27 points in Amsterdam and followed it with 33 against London before ending the regular season with 27 in Barcelona.

Jim Ballard receives instructions from the sideline

Those performances were enough to earn Ballard the starting job in the World Bowl and he didn't fail as the Claymores' 32 points were enough for glory. 'It was a really frustrating time being stuck on the sidelines in those early weeks,' he said. 'But that's the name of the game. There can only be 11 men on the field and if you're not one of them you have a responsibility not to show your disappointment. My main task was to help communicate the play calls to Steve so I was still very much involved. But when you have absolute confidence in your ability as a player it's always nice to get the chance to back up that belief by proving yourself out on the field. I think that self-confidence helped me keep my head up when I wasn't getting a game and I never doubted that my time would come.'

Ironically, Ballard's chance would have come sooner but for desperate timing on his part. Matthews went down injured in week six against Rhein Fire but as the fans at Murrayfield waited for Ballard to run out and replace, it was third-string Khari Jones who appeared. That was because Ballard was 3,000 miles away in Ohio, getting married to fiancée Erin. 'You couldn't have scripted that,' he admitted. 'It was actually two bits of bad luck, not one. The only reason I arranged my marriage for a weekend during the World League season was because I didn't expect to be involved this year.

Ballard against his old team, the London Monarchs

'When I was allocated to the Monarchs last year, I assumed I would be returning to the Bengals when the season ended and my involvement with the World League would be over. Of course, they went and cut me and suddenly everything was up in the air again. The date had already been set and there was nothing I could do to change it. I couldn't believe it when I got back to Scotland and learned Khari had got a play. I wait all season for a chance and he's been in the country two weeks and gets on the field!'

While Ballard took all the plaudits at the end of the season, it was tough not to feel sorry for Matthews. He stuck it out when he admits his own form was far from solid and laid the foundations for the Claymores' glory season. The 26-year-old had his finest moment in the pressure-cooker atmosphere of the Waldstadion as the Claymores earned the right to host the World Bowl. On a night when he could barely hear himself think as 32,000 fans bellowed their support for the Galaxy, Matthews kept ice-cool to pick out Sean LaChapelle for the vital touchdown. Add a crucial 38-yard pass to LaChapelle to set up an overtime win in the season opener at White Hart Lane, and it's easy to see where the Claymores' flying start was coming from.

Matthews passed for a total of 1,560 yards on the season to help fire a stuttering offence. 'It was disappointing to miss out in the end but you can't take it away from Jim,' he said. 'Once he got his chance, it was obvious there was going to be no way back for me because he was playing so well. I know how disappointed he was not to get the starting job but he gave me tremendous support and I like to think I did the same for him when he was in control.

'As far as I was concerned, every game after the first one against London was a bonus because I was so nervous on the first drive I could have cost us the game there and then. I blew all of our time-outs on the first series and you can't get a more horrible start than that. Thankfully, I settled down and got us through and I did a few things during the season which I am pretty proud of.

'For me, the highlight had to be that night in Frankfurt. It was such a massive achievement to go out there and win in front of that crowd, with all the noise they were making. I like to think I played my part in winning Scotland the World Bowl.'

Yo Murphy and Jim Ballard on the sidelines

Steve Livingstone and Andy Colvin

Jim Criner had watched his side struggle in the Claymores' last three regular season games, and, following the loss in Barcelona, faced a press conference to kick off World Bowl week. The Scots' opponents in the Bowl would be reigning champions Frankfurt Galaxy. If the Claymores were to win their first title, they would now have to regroup to defeat a team that had refound its early season form.

Although an unblemished record, with two epic triumphs, had been recorded against the Germans during the regular season there were doubts that any team – never mind one that seemed to have lost its intensity losing two out of its last three games – would manage three wins in a row over Ernie Stautner's crack troops. But Criner was certain his Claymores would bounce back. 'Our defence has been hurt with the loss of Ty Parten and Herman Carroll and we played without two of our key players in Mark Sander and George Coghill against Barcelona,' explained Criner. 'Our players are going to have to step up to the challenge this week. The two things you can do in this situation are sit down and feel sorry for yourself or step up and play. I expect our players now to step up and play. We have come too far, and worked too hard not to get what we have all been striving for – a World Bowl championship.'

Special teams captain and national player Ben Torriero was certain the players would rise to the challenge. 'Everybody knows the importance of this one,' said Ben. 'We'll practise hard this week. Coach Criner won't let us fail and I'm sure everyone will be ready to play come Sunday.' Fellow national Scott Couper was also looking forward to the big game. 'This is the most important game of my life,' said the former Glasgow Lion. 'I'm like the little boy who kicked a soccer ball around in the street and dreamed of one day playing for Scotland against England at Wembley. On Sunday, Murrayfield will be my Wembley.'

Preparations for the World League's showpiece finale had been going well and tickets were now selling at the rate of 1,000 per day. 'We had made rather ambitious estimates after we qualified in week five to host the game that we would sell 25,000 tickets for the World Bowl,' said Claymores general manager Mike Keller. 'But now I know we are going to have that number and may even see 15,000 more fans at the game than we expected.'

The Bowl would not only be played out in front of tens of thousands in the stadium. A global television audience of 200 million was expected to tune in too, with Fox Sports, one of America's premier sporting networks and co-funders of the league, broadcasting the game live to over 50 million homes in the United States. The World Bowl would also be beamed in 11 different languages to 126 countries world-wide, throughout Europe, to Australia, Central and South America and across parts of Asia, the Far East and Africa going out to twice as many viewers around the globe as had watched World Bowl 95.

With Scotland under the global sporting spotlight it was also going to be a big day at Murrayfield. A pre-game party was going to take place on an epic scale with Scottish rock

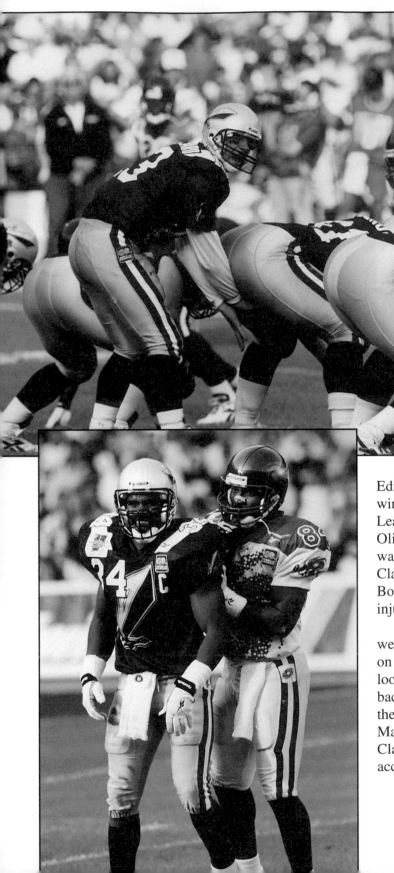

groups Gun and the Tartan Amoebas headlining. The University of Maryland Marching Band would also be on hand to add a traditional American sports flavour and would put on the half-time show while Scottish folk singer Ronnie Browne, member of The Corries, would sing late partner Roy Williamson's *Flower of Scotland* in front of a packed Murrayfield before kick-off.

On the field itself, nothing was being left to chance, with Murrayfield groundstaff re-sodding parts of the hallowed turf exclusively for the Bowl game and, after the paint on the field had dried with team and World Bowl colours, the national stadium was looking resplendent and all set to host its first World Bowl. With all that going on it would have been easy for the players to get distracted but Jim Criner was working his squad hard out at Stepps in preparation for the big game.

On the Tuesday before the game, as opponents Galaxy jetted in to Edinburgh, the Claymores swept the board, winning eight honours on the All-World League team announced by league president Oliver Luck in Glasgow. But the news wasn't all positive. Jared Kaaiohelo, the Claymores starting full-back, would miss the Bowl after suffering a season-ending knee injury in Barcelona.

By media day on Thursday the players were ready to play. Mingling with reporters on the track at Murrayfield both squads looked relaxed enough, but under the laid-back response to the many media questions, the tension was rising. Galaxy wide receiver Mario Bailey got into a bragging match with Claymores quarterback Jim Ballard after accusing the Scots of going soft after their

week-five clincher. 'We had to play our last two games knowing the loser was out. Sunday will be the same and I don't know if the Claymores are ready for that sort of war,' said Bailey. 'They've had it easy over the last five weeks because their games didn't matter. The Claymores have got the better of us twice this year, but it won't happen a third time.'

Ballard hit back, saying: 'If Frankfurt want to think that way then that's up to them, but it's just rubbish. How can he say we've had easy games when the sides in this league have so little between them?' And Claymores offensive tackle Keith Wagner added: 'There has been a kind of electricity about practice this week which has maybe been missing since we clinched the World Bowl place. I don't care what Frankfurt say – we'll be ready. Every guy on this team is focused on what we have to do.' But Bailey retorted: 'They are not going to find it so easy to pick their game up a notch to face us. We have the best receivers in the league and we're due to catch their defence out at some point.'

To win the Bowl the Claymores would, once again, have to stop that receiving corps of Bailey, Mike Bellamy, Gary Harrell and, perhaps most dangerous of all, Jay Kearney. They would also have to put considerable pressure on Galaxy's veteran passer Steve Pelluer, back in the starting spot after a mid-season slump and the loss of Brad Bretz due to injury. The Claymores would also be facing an old friend in quarterback Terry Karg, drafted in to replace Bretz as back-up to Pelluer.

The Germans had suffered since their week-five loss to the Claymores, but had picked up to win their last two games and, following their 28–20 victory over Amsterdam, looked now to be firing on all cylinders. 'We have gone through a lot of adversity this season,' said Galaxy head coach Ernie Stautner. 'But our character has come through and the players have raised the level of their game despite our troubles. The Scottish Claymores are the best team in the league right now. We've been studying hard this week to get to the level we need to be at to win because the Claymores are beatable, but we will have to play the best game of the season to do it.'

To combat the Galaxy offensive threat the Claymores boasted the World League's best defensive secondary led by safeties George Coghill and James Fuller, but the key contest was going to be at the cornerback position and how well James Williams and Forey Duckett would handle the Galaxy receivers. The Scots offence, on the arm of Jim Ballard, had been improving steadily since the disappointment in Amsterdam, and with their own dangerous receiving corps in Sean LaChapelle, Yo Murphy and Scott Couper, they knew exactly how to exploit Galaxy's hot and cold defensive secondary.

Siran Stacy, the league's best running back, would have to have another record day but would only be allowed to do so if his offensive line, featuring Purvis Hunt, Keith Wagner and Lance Zeno, could manhandle Galaxy hard-hitters Don Reynolds and Tom Cavallo.

If it turned out to be close, both sides, in Claymores' Paul McCallum and Galaxy's Ralf Kleinmann, had kickers capable of long-range, match-winning kicks. 'The sides are pretty evenly matched,' said James Fuller. 'Once we get over the initial nerves and things settle down one side is going to have to emerge as the dominant force if it isn't going to go down to the wire.' Galaxy passer Pelluer warned: 'It's no secret that we are a passing team. That's how we've been successful in the past and that's what we're going to have to do to win the World Bowl.'

WORLD BOWL 96: CLAYMORES ON TOP OF THE WORLD
Scottish Claymores 32 v. Frankfurt Galaxy 27

The sun shone and the fans came out in force for the World Bowl. Crowds averaging 9,000 had watched the Scots struggle through the '95 season, but on this super Sunday all that was forgotten as almost 40,000 packed the backfields for an afternoon of pre-match partying. As the crowds enjoyed the pre-game festivities, the atmosphere was tense inside the locker rooms under Murrayfield's West Stand as both teams prepared for the biggest game of the year. An emotional rendition of *Flower of Scotland* by Ronnie Browne had the huge crowd fired up come game time at six o'clock, and the start of the match was to prove as dramatic as the blast from Edinburgh Castle's one o'clock gun which fired to start the game.

The Claymores had won the coin toss but head coach Jim Criner had chosen to kick the ball to Galaxy to pressure the Frankfurt offence off the bat. Gavin Hastings struck a deep kick to get the game under way. Wide receiver Mario Bailey, who'd been so outspoken in the run-up to the game, fielded the kick at Frankfurt's ten-yard line and began his return. But he only got as far as the 25-yard line when George Coghill flew in from his kick-off coverage position to swipe the ball from Bailey's grasp. Markus Thomas, who had sprinted downfield hoping to make the tackle, was rewarded with an even bigger prize as the ball popped out of Bailey's hands and into his.

There was no one between Thomas and the endzone 22 yards away and, as the crowd erupted, the running back sped across the goal line to record the fastest touchdown in World League history. With 11 seconds gone the Claymores had made a dream start to their dream final. Hastings, so often the hero at Murrayfield, converted his 'kick-off' PAT and Scotland took a 7–0 lead.

Reigning champions Frankfurt weren't going to crumble without a fight, and retained their composure to get on the scoreboard on their next possession. After Hastings's restart kick Pelluer marshalled an 11-play drive, capped with a 16-yard reverse play run into the endzone by receiver Jay Kearney. Ralf Kleinmann was solid on the extra point and the scores were tied at seven with six minutes gone.

Things were looking grim

GAME STATISTICS

WORLD BOWL 96: FRANKFURT GALAXY at SCOTTISH CLAYMORES; MURRAYFIELD, EDINBURGH; 23 JUNE 1996; ATT: 38,982; WEATHER: SUNNY, 20°C

SCORE BY PERIODS

	1	2	3	4	
GALAXY	7	7	6	7	27
CLAYMORES	7	12	9	4	32

SCORING SUMMARY

Team	Period	Elapsed Time	Play	Score
Sco	1st	0:11	TD, Thomas fumble return (Hastings PAT)	0-7
Fra	1st	6:27	TD, Kearney 16 run (Kleinmann PAT)	7-7
Fra	2nd	4:39	TD, Bailey 2 pass Pelluer (Kleinmann PAT)	14-7
Sco	2nd	14:09	TD, Murphy 6 pass Ballard (PAT missed)	14-13
Sco	2nd	14:52	TD, Murphy 16 pass Ballard (2PAT failed)	14-19
Sco	3rd	6:46	FG, McCallum 46	14-22
Fra	3rd	9:02	TD, Bailey 32 pass Pelluer (2PAT failed)	20-22
Sco	3rd	8:42	TD, Murphy 71 pass Ballard (PAT missed)	20-28
Sco	4th	5:06	FG, McCallum 50 (4 points)	20-32
Fra	4th	12:10	TD, Bellamy 5 pass Pelluer (Kleinmann PAT)	27-32

TEAM STATISTICS

	GALAXY	CLAYMORES
First Downs	21	14
Rushes/Yards	23/69	25/54
Net Passing Yards	244	252
Total Net Yards	336	306
Passing (A-C-I)	37/24/1	29/17/0
Punts/Average	6/44.6	6/34.5
Fumbles/Lost	4/2	5/2
Penalties	11/70	7/60
Time of Possession	31:07	28:53

INDIVIDUAL STATISTICS

RUSHING
Galaxy: Seibert 12-31; Phillips 7-17; Pelluer 3-5; Kearney 1-16
Claymores: Stacy 22-49; Ballard 3-5

PASSING
Galaxy: Pelluer 37-24-267, 3TD, 1INT
Claymores: Ballard: 29-17-263, 3TD, 0INT

RECEIVING
Galaxy: Kearney 3-23; Phillips 1-4; Smith 1-8; Harrell 4-73; Harrison 1-13; Seibert 1-(-3); Bailey 8-104-2; Bellamy 4-36-1; Bender 1-9
Claymores: Tate 4-49; LaChapelle 1-11; Murphy 7-163-3; Stacy 2-8; Couper 2-25; Dickerson 1-7

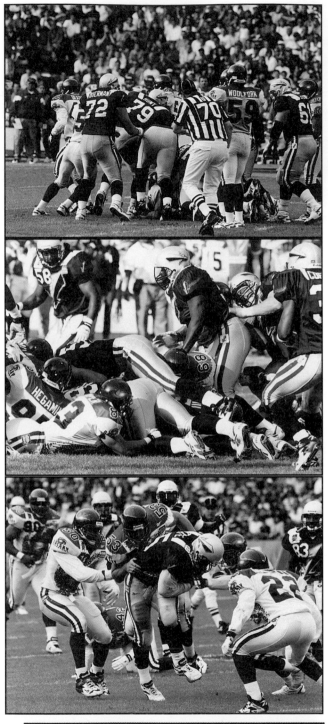

Middle: Jerold Jeffcoat in the middle of it all

Bottom: Four Galaxy players are needed to take down Tate

for the Claymores when, at the start of the second quarter, star receiver Sean LaChapelle crumpled to the ground in agony after pulling his groin on a simple 'in' route. The league-leading receiver and MVP was carried off the field, his World Bowl dream wrecked, leaving the Claymores to battle the rest of the match minus their biggest offensive threat.

The Scots were forced to punt and tragedy turned to farce when safety David Wilson almost picked off Pelluer, only to watch in horror as his tipped interception deflected into the waiting hands of Galaxy receiver Gary Harrell at the Claymores' one-yard line. Two plays later Mario Bailey made amends for his opening blunder, beating James Williams's coverage to catch Pelluer's two-yard pass in the corner of the endzone for Galaxy's second score. Kleinmann made the extra point and Frankfurt were in charge at 14–7.

Luck seemed to have deserted the Claymores when, on their next drive, Siran Stacy uncharacteristically fumbled the ball which was recovered by Galaxy linebacker Tom Cavallo. But Frankfurt could not take advantage of the mistake, and with the first-half two-minute warning approaching, the Claymores pulled themselves together. Once again the Braveheart defence pinned their ears back and pushed Frankfurt deep in their own territory, Bryan Proby sacking Pelluer at his one-yard line, forcing Kevin Feighery to punt out of his own endzone.

His poor kick was fumbled by Markus Thomas but picked up by David Wilson at midfield and returned 12 yards to Galaxy's 39-yard line. With 1:39 left in the half Jim Ballard launched a 38-yard pass to Yo Murphy and the little receiver stepped out of Sean LaChapelle's shadow to catch it at Galaxy's one-yard line. Siran Stacy then lost five yards, swamped by the Galaxy defence, but on the next play it was Murphy on the receiving end of Ballard's pass again, this

Joe O'Brien celebrates a sack

Injured Sean LaChapelle leaves the pitch

time in the corner of the endzone for a six-yard touchdown score. Hastings missed the extra point to leave the Scots 14–13 behind but the half was to end as dramatically as it had begun.

Paul McCallum launched a deep restart kick which was caught by Mike Bellamy. But again, the returner's curse was to strike and Bellamy, ironically on to replace the disgraced Bailey, fumbled the ball which was recovered by Claymores linebacker Shannon Jones at Frankfurt's 15-yard line. With 13 seconds remaining in the half Jim Ballard rolled left and lobbed a pass towards Yo Murphy in the corner of the endzone. The pass was a little overthrown but Murphy made a supreme effort to record a stunning one-handed catch, while keeping his

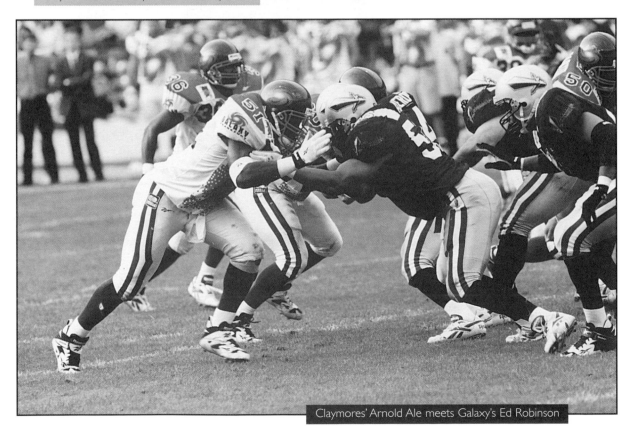
Claymores' Arnold Ale meets Galaxy's Ed Robinson

feet in the endzone, to punish Galaxy and put the Claymores in front. Ballard's attempted two-point conversion pass fell incomplete and the Claymores went into the locker room 19–14 in front but, more importantly, with Murphy's late strikes, in command of a huge psychological edge.

McCallum added to the Scots' tally, booting a 46-yard field goal at the start of the third quarter but Frankfurt rallied with Mario Bailey outrunning the coverage of old friend James Williams to catch a 32-yard touchdown pass from Pelluer two minutes later. The Claymores wasted no time in hitting back, though, as the thrilling shoot-out continued. On the first play after Frankfurt's score Jim Ballard dropped back and hit Murphy with a ten-yard pass, but the receiver jinked past coverman Cecil Doggette and scampered down the sidelines and into the endzone on an amazing 71-yard touchdown play.

Hastings wasn't having a field day, missing his second extra point, but Paul McCallum was, confidently booting through a massive 50-yard kick for four points and a 32–20 lead at the start of the fourth quarter. Galaxy weren't going to relinquish their crown so easily, though, and Pelluer once again found Bellamy on a five-yard touchdown pass with three minutes remaining to set up a thrilling finale, the Germans behind 27–32.

The Claymores stalled on their next possession and had to punt giving Frankfurt one last chance to win the game with 59 seconds left. But the match was to end on a controversial note when Galaxy rusher Ingo Seibert fumbled the ball short of the first down marker on a desperate fourth-down play. With the rules banning a fumble from being advanced in the last two minutes of the game the officials ruled the ball dead, handing the crucial possession back to the Claymores with only 19 seconds remaining. All Jim Ballard had to do was fall to a knee and the Claymores were crowned World Bowl kings, the 38,982 crowd inside Murrayfield erupting joyously on the final whistle.

Jim Criner led his squad up the steps of the West Stand at Murrayfield to receive the World Bowl trophy from NFL president Neil Austrian and World League president Oliver Luck. Criner had turned his team around from worst to first and, after raising the crystal globe above his head to the delight of the huge crowd and saluting victory with his now traditional post-match press conference battle cry of 'How 'Bout Them Claymores!', the coach said: 'The fans did their part today. The twelfth man really made a big difference in the football game and it meant a great deal for our football players to win today, not only for themselves but, with the bond they've built up with the supporters, the fans here in Scotland. I can't begin to tell you how great this is.'

And the triumphant head coach added: 'It's been a hallmark of this team all year that when a big name player goes out the way Sean LaChapelle did today, our back-up members of the team step up and become heroes. That's just what happened with Yo Murphy.' Murphy, now crowned the hero of the hour and awarded the World Bowl MVP honours for his seven-catch, 163-yard and three-touchdown game-winning performance, said: 'I've been waiting for this moment my whole life. My second touchdown catch was the best I have ever made – I knew it was a touchdown as soon as I got one hand on the ball.

'All credit to Jim Ballard for laying it on the money for me. I feel very sorry for Sean though. No one likes to see that kind of thing happen – especially in the World Bowl. I've got to give him huge thanks also. When he was injured he told me that this was my big chance and to go out and do it. That gave me the confidence to step up and fill Sean's shoes.'

Hastings, Torriero and Couper admire the World Bowl trophy

And Scott Couper, after seeing his World Bowl dream realised, added: 'This was my Super Bowl. I'm so proud to be a part of this team and this organisation. It was a dream come true to stand in front of that crowd singing *Flower of Scotland*. It was a thrilling match and I'm still numb – I can't believe we've actually won the World Bowl.'

YO MURPHY: CATCHING A DREAM

As a kid growing up in San Pedro, California, Yo Murphy quickly got used to being a no-name sort of guy. Christened Llewellyn Murphy, his Christian name was quickly dropped when his little sister found it too much of a mouthful to pronounce. The name Yo-Yo was adopted instead and it quickly became shortened to Yo.

It was that name which was on everyone's lips at Murrayfield on 23 June as Murphy's

'HOW 'BOUT THEM CLAYMORES!'

Law decreed the Claymores would become World League champs and Frankfurt would head home minus their trophy. Despite achieving hero status with his three World Bowl touchdowns, Murphy had to wait a long time before becoming the darling of the fans. Much of his regular season was spent living in the shadows of fellow wide receiver Sean LaChapelle and running back Siran Stacy as they powered the Claymores towards the Murrayfield show-piece.

But one glance at the season's stats proves Murphy wasn't simply along for the ride. That memorable World Bowl performance took his season's touchdown tally to eight, one more than LaChapelle and just one behind points machine Stacy. It also meant he completed the job he had started way back in week one, when he opened the Claymores' account for the season with a touchdown against the London Monarchs at White Hart Lane. But Murphy's not bitter about being the forgotten man for much of the season. Instead he prefers it that way.

'It was never going to be any other way because Sean and Siran were playing such great football,' said the 25-year-old. 'To be honest, I'm not that comfortable with people singing my praises anyway. I'd rather just get on with the job and let someone else do the talking to the media and all that stuff. The weird thing was that Sean hated all the attention just as much as I would have so in a way I was really lucky that the focus was on him.'

Yo Murphy ready to run

That focus switched dramatically during the World Bowl as LaChapelle limped out of the action early in the second quarter with a damaged groin muscle. But as the going got tough, Yo got going. His stunning one-handed catch to give the Claymores a half-time lead will never be forgotten by those lucky enough to witness it. It will certainly never be forgotten by Murphy.

'That was one of those moments you think will never happen to you,' he said. 'You're out there in a championship game, scrapping and fighting for any little advantage, and suddenly in one moment you become the hero. It's something every kid dreams about and I just feel very privileged that the chance came my way. It was by far the best catch I have ever made on a football field.'

Murphy's World Bowl heroics would have come as no surprise to the students of the stats, as he ran into a rich seam of form at the end of the season. While the Claymores struggled as the World Bowl loomed, Murphy simply got better and better. Four touchdowns in the last three regular season games served notice the receiver was ready to move in. And Murphy insisted there was a perfectly good reason for his late form surge. 'I struggled in the middle of the season because I wasn't fully fit,' he said. 'I picked up a couple of niggling injuries and the nature of our game means you simply don't have the chance to rest up and recover.

'We also had problems with another receiver, Lee Gissendaner. He was struggling with a shoulder injury so we were kind of doing half a job each to help the team out as best we could. I don't have any problem with that, it's the nature of football. You just have to suck up the pain and get on with the job. Quitters win no prizes in this sport.'

That Murphy is no quitter was never in doubt. In week three he chased an apparently hopeless cause to dive full length and produce another from his repertoire of stunning catches. That reception set up Scott Couper's first-ever touchdown for the Claymores and Murphy admitted he took as much pleasure from that moment as from any of his own touchdowns. 'Until I made the catch in the World Bowl that reception was probably the greatest of my career,' he said. 'But the big thrill for me that day was seeing Scoops's reaction when he got into the endzone.

'The receivers all hung around together off the field so I knew how badly he wanted to score that first touchdown and how desperate he was that it should happen at Murrayfield in front of his own countrymen. When I saw him celebrating I was just so pleased for him. I think in that moment I really understood just how much the Claymores meant to the people of Scotland.'

THE ALL-WORLD LEAGUE TEAM

The strength and success of the World League-champion Claymores was reflected in the World League's end-of-season awards announced during World Bowl week. No less than eight Claymores players, including star receiver Sean LaChapelle and top-rated running back Siran Stacy, were nominated by Europe's media to the World League's All-Star team, and to cap what had been a remarkable season for head coach Jim Criner, in which he turned his team around from worst to first, the Claymores play-caller was named Coach of the Year.

'It's great to have so many players named, especially the way in which the voting was done among Europe's media. It means a lot to know that our players have caught the eye all over Europe this season,' said Criner. League president Oliver Luck made the announcement. Along with the eight Claymores, six players from Amsterdam Admirals, five from London Monarchs, three from Rhein Fire and one from Barcelona were named to the 1996 squad. The Claymores' World Bowl opponents Frankfurt had four players nominated. Ironically, Criner replaced Galaxy head coach Ernie Stautner as Coach of the Year.

LaChapelle, the Kansas City Chiefs allocated receiver who led the World League in receiving with 1,023 yards, was also named Most Valuable Offensive Player of the Year – chosen by the six World League coaches – pipping fellow Claymore Stacy, who led the league in touchdowns and rushing. More remarkable, though, was the selection of another Claymore, the club's No.1 draft choice Ty Parten, as Defensive MVP. Parten, who missed the World Bowl after suffering a season-ending knee injury, was not named in the All-Star team and had only played in half of the Claymores' regular season games. However, the opposition coaches around the league rated his limited impact so highly, he was the automatic choice for the award.

The strength of the Claymores offence was mirrored in the selections of one half of the Scots' offensive line in centre Lance Zeno, guard Purvis Hunt and tackle Keith Wagner to the league-best squad. The Claymores' highly successful safety partnership of George Coghill and James Fuller were also honoured, as was defensive tackle Jerold Jeffcoat – all named to the All-World League defence.

ALL-WORLD LEAGUE TEAM

OFFENCE
QUARTERBACK - Will Furrer (Amsterdam)
RUNNING BACKS - Siran Stacy (Scotland), Tony Vinson (London)
WIDE RECEIVERS - Sean LaChapelle (Scotland), Phillip Bobo (Amsterdam)
TIGHT END - Byron Chamberlain (Rhein)
TACKLES - Keith Wagner (Scotland), George Hegamin (Frankfurt)
GUARDS - Purvis Hunt (Scotland), Marcus Spears (Amsterdam)
CENTRE - Lance Zeno (Scotland)
NATIONAL PLAYER - Ingo Seibert (Frankfurt)
OFFENSIVE MVP: Sean LaChapelle (Scotland)

DEFENCE
ENDS - Jon Baker (Frankfurt), Jerry Drake (London)
TACKLES - Blaine Berger (London), Jerold Jeffcoat (Scotland)
LINEBACKERS - Rico Mack (Amsterdam), Tom Cavallo (Frankfurt), Percy Snow (Rhein)
CORNERBACKS - Kenny McEntyre (London), Kelly Sims (Amsterdam)
SAFETIES - George Coghill (Scotland), James Fuller (Scotland)
NATIONAL PLAYER - Lewis Capes (London)
DEFENSIVE MVP: Ty Parten (Scotland)

SPECIALISTS
KICKER - Scott Szeredy (Barcelona)
PUNTER - Leo Araguz (Rhein)
RETURNER - T.C. Wright (Amsterdam)

COACH OF THE YEAR
Jim Criner (Scotland)

Half-time performance by the Weir Scottish Claymores cheerleaders

THE CHEERLEADERS by Dawn Peterson

Yo Murphy crossed the goal line for the third time during the World Bowl and the crowd erupted into an arm-raising roar. On this particular day at Murrayfield, the girls in blue and white would not have to work as hard to get the attending audience involved. For the Scottish Claymores cheerleaders during the championship match, the job was pure enjoyment – although it had not always been that way.

Cheerleader Laura Mair

Half of this year's cheerleaders have returned from the 1995 squad, and they could tell you about a day when going out to dance in front of a crowd at a Claymores match was not so glamorous. 'Jumping about in front of 10,000 people in the pouring rain with your hair glued to your head, cheering on a football team that could do nothing but lose every match played on home ground, was not exactly what I had pictured the job of a cheerleader to be like,' said Debbie Jackson in respect of her first season cheering for the team. 'If you didn't have a sense of humour before you joined the Claymores' cheerleading squad, you sure learned quick how to find one.'

Debbie, from Glasgow, came out for the 1995 trials on assignment from *The Daily Record*. Instead of just writing about the experience of becoming a professional cheerleader, she made the team and got the chance actually to live out the role. 'Being a Claymores cheerleader for the past two years had given me the chance to participate in many fun things that I would not normally be doing. Being on television and performing at venues all over Scotland has allowed me to act out the alternative [although some would probably say that they've seen the side long before] extrovert side of my personality. And the job perks? I can't remember the last time I paid to get into a club in Glasgow!'

The tough road for the girls at the beginning was not always due to supporting a losing team. The words 'bimbo' and 'sexist' kept cropping up in reference to the novel team of dancers, which seemed pretty unjust to a group of girls studying law, physiotherapy and sports management, writing for national newspapers, teaching classes, and so on. Second-year cheerleader Pamela Don pointed out the fact that 'performing as a cheerleader in public is no different from performing on stage as a dancer, which many of us have been doing for years'. Once people saw that the girls were professional dancers, coupled with the number of appearances that they make throughout the year (some paid, but many for charity), the associated words faded away into the land of misconception.

It is obvious – due to the 95 per cent return of the 1995 squad to this year's team – that the girls had a great experience throughout their inaugural year, and although the Claymores football team ranked last, the cheerleaders were voted No. 1 in the World League by the British Cheerleading Association. Another veteran, Siobhan Young from Edinburgh, saw her involvement with the cheerleaders as a self-expanding venture. 'People's reactions at promotions, along with the crowd's appreciation at matches, has been a real confidence-builder. Being with the squad had enabled me to meet lots of people, in addition to forming friendships with the other girls on the team. Working together as a team has also been a great experience; it's not just the players who have to learn how to perform in this capacity.'

Much of the girls' teamwork attitude was developed by their choreographer from the LA/Oakland Raiderettes, Ramona Braganza. Ramona, born in Germany and schooled in Canada, came on to the Claymores' scene in November of 1995 to conduct the first set of trials. The result was a squad of 20 girls from the Edinburgh and Glasgow areas, who were then trained by Ramona, two to three times a week, leading up to the season. The following year's tryouts saw an even bigger response, and the squad was increased to 30. When interviewed during the auditions, Ramona commented: 'The level of dance ability is very high this year, and the enthusiasm that I have seen today is very encouraging. Some of these girls would definitely be in contention for the Raiderette trials back in the States.'

Over the past two years, Ramona has flown to Scotland to train the fledgling Claymore cheerleaders, then back to the States to participate herself on the Raiderettes dance squad during the NFL season. It is easy to see the rightful pride she takes in 'her Scottish girls'. 'It is extremely rewarding to have been a part of something unknown from the beginning, and see it successfully take on the shape that you have worked so hard to mould it into. I couldn't begin to count the number of compliments I have received on how professional the girls look when they are performing out there on the pitch.'

The level of professionalism is carried off the field and into the everyday promotions and appearances that the girls participate in during the off-season. Unlike the players, the cheerleaders' role is a year-round one, involving many television, radio, video and personal appearances. Over the past couple of years the girls have appeared on STV's *Chartbite* and *Late Edition*, Channel 4's *Tribe TV* and BBC's *Mega Mag*. They have also performed at Ibrox Stadium, Celtic Park, Tynecastle and Easter Road, and have made a rock video with pop stars Fish and Sam Brown. In total the girls have turned out on approximately 200 occasions, around a quarter of them being charity-related. The amount of promotional exposure that the cheerleaders have given to the Claymores is immeasurable.

So, after the roar of the crowd has died down and the World Bowl trophy has been put away on display, it is the cheerleaders who will keep on going during the long off-season to make certain that the Claymores stay alive in the public's mind and the crowds return to Murrayfield for the 1997 season.

4. THE COACH'S STORY

Steve Livingstone

Jim Criner, the man who turned the Claymores' fortunes around from worst to first, never rests. Or so it seems. Just hours after directing his Scottish Claymores to World Bowl glory at Murrayfield – and in the process placing gridiron firmly on Scotland's sporting map – the head coach was already planning the 1997 season campaign in defence of his adopted nation's newest sporting title.

The coach spent most of the morning after the Bowl game answering his telephone, red hot with enquiries from NFL team scouts and coaches who had watched the World Bowl live on Fox Sports in the US and wanted to know more about key players in his championship squad.

Following the triumph Criner did take a short time out to reflect on what has been a truly remarkable season for his Claymores, and, in doing so, revealed that the challenge for next season – of becoming the first World League team successfully to defend its title – had already been taken up. 'No one in World League history has ever repeated. That's something that would be very special and is obviously going to be our challenge for next year,' said Criner. 'The players and coaches have already talked about it. We've already raised our sights and now the challenge has to be to repeat.'

Not that the World League Coach of the Year could, or would want to, ease off and rest on the laurels of success. He already tried that back in 1986 when he 'retired' from gridiron following a highly successful college coaching career in which he guided Idaho's Division 1AA Boise State University to four conference titles, three NCAA finals and one national championship, to concentrate on building a fishing supply business with his wife Ann in West Yellowstone, Montana.

Criner, also a world-class fly fisherman, spent six years on the river turning his business venture into another success story, but the lure and excitement of the gridiron proved too much – he admits 'I'm just one of those guys who has the football fever' – and he returned to coach in the developing World League with California's Sacramento Surge, in the days when the league had six teams in the United States as well as four in Europe.

The winning continued and, along with current Claymores general manager Mike Keller – manager of Sacramento at the time – Criner helped Surge pick up the World Bowl as an assistant coach in 1992. But the 30-year coaching veteran knows the despair of defeat too. The Claymores' inaugural campaign in 1995 saw him hold together a disfunctional team *en route* to a 2–8 season, after picking up the pieces following the dismissal of Lary Kuharich, the team's first head coach, just five days before Scotland's first game.

That season was, in Criner's eyes, an aberration, and despite the achievement of valiantly keeping the ship afloat for ten weeks, he was personally mortified and made a promise that the team he would field this year would be a completely different proposition. That promise, to give Scotland a team of winners, was honoured on 23 June when the head coach and his players raised the crystal globe at Murrayfield.

Although the rise to glory was complete, the head coach admitted there were a few hurdles to be negotiated along the way, none more so than in the week leading up to the World Bowl. 'After watching Frankfurt come back to eliminate Amsterdam in the final week of the regular season I was concerned,' admitted Criner. 'We'd just come off a disappointing defeat in Barcelona and our team was finding it tough to maintain its intensity.

Head coach Jim Criner instructs quarterback Steve Matthews

I thought we would be facing Amsterdam in the final. We had prepared for both but wanted to play the Admirals because of what happened in week eight. We also wanted to avoid Frankfurt because it's much tougher trying to beat a team three times in a row. But their win in Amsterdam really made us sit up and take notice. It told us that this football team was back and had rebounded from their mid-season slump.'

As his team endeavoured to refocus after arriving back from Spain, Criner sat down and watched the game film from Amsterdam – and did not like what he saw. 'Two things were of great concern to us,' said the coach. 'Number one you could see Pelluer was very healthy

and back on form – his confidence and experience were really showing. Secondly, they had to make an eight-play goal-line stand to stop Amsterdam – and they did it with their defensive end Don Reynolds coming up to make the big play.'

In the end, Criner's worst fears were not realised and it was the Claymores who were to come up with all the big plays on that glorious evening at Murrayfield. The head coach looked back on what turned out to be the most thrilling match of the entire World League season. 'It ended up being a game of big plays,' said Criner. 'But fortunately for us we had the players who could make the big plays. From the spectators' standpoint it was one of the most exciting games of the season, but as a coach you don't want to go through too many like that. It was a game where our players wanted to win in the worst way. They had prepared hard to win but a couple of our key players – Siran Stacy being the most notable – were over-ready. They were so tense they just didn't play their normal game.'

And the head coach revealed: 'We had told our players all week in practice that we could beat Frankfurt deep. When Sean went down in the second quarter there was some doubt whether we could continue to do that but we had Yo Murphy who ended up stepping up and having a big game. We knew we could hurt them with the play-action because they had their two safeties playing up close against the run. Fortunately, with Yo's speed, we were able to take advantage of this. It was fortunate that we made so many big plays but also that we

Defensive co-ordinator Ray Willsey

played so well on special teams, giving us that first early touchdown and putting us in a great field position for two more.

'The week before, against Barcelona, our special teams play was awful. We'd also lost Jared Kaaiohelo and Robert Flickinger, but we were able to shuffle personnel around and we had seen some weaknesses on their special teams where they would kick the ball to one place. Again, we were fortunate to be able to take advantage of this and worked hard on the special teams aspect of our game in the run-in to the World Bowl.'

But the Claymores didn't have things all their own way. 'Frankfurt did an excellent job of controlling the short passing game,' admitted the coach. 'Without Ty Parten and Herman Carroll we were not as dominant a defence as we had been. Defensively they also did such a good job of taking our run game away. To compensate we were able to run just enough to keep them honest but went deep more often. We felt, as the game unfolded, that we needed big plays because we weren't going to have the consistent running game we had all year, because Frankfurt shut it down. We also made some adjustments at half-time that paid off for us. The other thing was that if the game went to a shoot-out, I felt we could win it. It was a calculated gamble but it paid off.'

The coach highlighted an unsung hero of the day who, in his eyes, played as vital a role as Jim Ballard or Yo Murphy. 'If we had to depend on a field goal to win it I knew Paul McCallum would do it for us,' said Criner. 'In the end we didn't need a last second kick but Paul's two field goals – from 46 and 50 yards – were pivotal. Adding up to seven points they were the equivalent to one of our running backs running 96 yards for a touchdown.'

Criner also laid credit for the victory on his backroom staff, the hand-picked coaches who showed their considerable talent and ability in being able to readjust their personnel and gameplans to every situation. It was a staff that Criner worked hard to assemble in the off-season. Between them his assistant coaches and co-ordinators had accrued over 160 years' coaching experience and had won a combined 30-plus titles, including Super Bowls, World Bowls and national championships. 'The coaching staff we managed to assemble this season had an incredibly impressive pedigree,' said Criner.

Rejoining Criner for yet another campaign, and his second in Scotland, was long-time friend, 'drill sergeant' line coach Bill Dutton. Dutton's experience spans over four decades, beginning at the University of California, Davis in 1954. Dutton also coached at Cal State and California-Berkeley before sandwiching stints in the USFL and Canadian Football League with two years at Division 1AA Boise State alongside Criner. His ability to develop the Claymores' hard-hitting defence not only resulted in a good defence but also a good offence, Criner's offence linemen having to face the crack unit in every practice. Dutton's influence also extended beyond the trenches, his skill to motivate inspiring the whole team.

That Cal-Davis connection continued in the appointment of offensive co-ordinator Jim Sochor. Sochor, considered an offensive genius by his peers, won 18 straight league championships while at UC Davis – a feat unchallenged in NCAA history – from which he compiled an amazing 156 wins, 41 losses and five ties with a staggering conference record of 92–5. In recognition of his achievement Sochor was named Division II National Coach of the Year in 1983. Along with that incredible record Sochor brought an exciting brand of offence inspired by the legendary head coach of the San Francisco 49ers, Bill Walsh, known simply as the West Coast Offence.

A quiet and unassuming man, Sochor's aim was exact. 'Our goals and philosophy this season were attached to utilising the ability of each of the six skill positions on the offence. We kept the plays simple but moved our running backs, wide receivers and tight ends around in order to take advantage of mismatches on defence. The system was designed to confuse the defence by disguising the plays – and for that reason we used a lot of different sets and motions this year. We were looking for the worst defenders to be left covering our best players. And nine times out of ten that's what we got. You've seen how devastating that was when you watched a receiver like Sean LaChapelle come up with huge catches game after game.'

Sochor's Midas touch and hard-work ethic were equalled by that of legendary defensive co-ordinator Ray Willsey – the catalyst in bringing glory to Scotland. Fans of the World League knew all about Willsey's background. After 18 years coaching in the NFL, including ten years at Oakland Raiders, he picked up his 'Minister of Defence' nickname as London Monarchs' defensive co-ordinator the year they won the first ever World Bowl at Wembley in 1991. After another year in London, this time as Monarchs head coach, Willsey moved on to Frankfurt where, in 1995, he was once again the defensive play-caller on a World Bowl-winning team.

Coming to Scotland, Willsey promised to install an uncompromising defence. 'It will be, quite simply a stop-'em defence,' said the defensive guru. 'The basic philosophy is to assemble players who can pursue but who can also bring the big hit – hitting hard is how you dominate. I call it the run and hit defence.'

That is exactly what he delivered as the Claymores' 'Highland Sting' became the top-rated defensive unit in the first half of the season and, almost single-handedly, helped the Claymores to at least half of their regular season wins, including that week-five showdown in Frankfurt where the Galaxy quarterbacks were raided for five interceptions and three sacks. No team found it easy to win the week after facing Willsey's defence. Seven times teams lost their next game after facing the Bravehearts – perhaps the most telling statistic of the season.

Helping Willsey and Dutton to develop that hard-hitting defence was linebackers coach Larry Owens. A native Californian, Owens starred as a defensive tackle at Cal State-Fullerton. His physical stature was matched by his considerable coaching experience: 17 years at San Mateo College, where he turned a losing programme into a three championship 34–15–2 winner.

Sochor was assisted by two relatively young coaches whose footballing intelligence went hand in hand with an intense enthusiasm for the game. Vince Alcalde, who, like Criner, began his career at Boise State, received plaudits for his expert handling of the receivers, among them national player Scott Couper. And last, but certainly by no means least, was national coach Mike Kenny, now the longest-serving coach on the Claymores staff. His experiences from the '95 season, and a busy off-season which saw the former Glasgow Lions running back establish a youth development programme for Scotland with nationwide coaching clinics, saw Mike bringing even more to the Claymores in his new role as running backs coach.

Remarkably, Criner's seeds for World Bowl glory were sown the day after the 1995 nightmare ended. As he assembled his coaching staff, Criner wrote to a handful of key players he wanted to invite back, explaining what would be expected of them in achieving the World League title. That painstaking pre-planning, which reaped this season's reward, has already begun again in shaping next year's campaign. Criner has again sent out the players' letters – first to thank his victors but also to establish the new goals for next season.

The head coach will continue to be busy throughout the off-season and ahead lies six months recruitment and 'scouting' – visits to various NFL pre-season training camps and

Criner cheers his team on to the pitch

matches not only to touch base and give moral support to the many Claymores who will undoubtably make the top grade this year following their World League success, but also to spot possible replacements for those same players he will lose to big-buck NFL contracts.

Recruiting and scouting prowess is something Criner was renowned for in his college days and something he sees as crucial if the Claymores are to be the first team to 'repeat'. 'One of the nicest things about this year was when the players, to a man, all said they wanted to come back to Scotland if they didn't make it onto an NFL team. Hopefully I'll get a chance to see as many of them as possible in the training camps but I'll also be looking at possible replacements and will also catch up with a number of players we identified last season but who ended up not playing in the league.'

With nearly half his team on the verge of breaking into the NFL, Criner will, no doubt, be left with a big hole and a headache for next season. In exchange, the coach will be allowed a protection of up to 15 of his starters from this year who don't make the NFL grade. Criner says he will also 'take in' a number of the top college all-star games around December to view any fresh talent that may become available in the World League draft next February – but each year brings the additional task of rebuilding a team almost from scratch. It all adds to the challenge for the 56-year-old play-caller.

'Because we won the league this year we will have to draft last, so the scouting procedure and allocation programmes become very, very important – even more so than last year. Like last year, we'll be looking to identify the bulk of next year's team before the draft so we can key in on specific areas to strengthen our team, rather than draft across the board.'

Looking back on a glorious season which Criner describes as 'the greatest thrill of his coaching career' – eclipsing even the national championship he won in similar circumstances with Boise State in 1980 (a losing division two team which Criner turned around, beating four 1A teams *en route* to the title) – two things will stay with him long after the lustre on his second World Bowl ring has dulled. 'The thing that I will remember most from this season is the kind of football team we had. When we came from behind against London in the first game of the season, I said afterwards that we had a chance to win every game we were in. That's the first time I knew the true character of our team and it was then I believed we could go all the way. Unfortunately you don't get a group of players together like that very often. Apart from the last week of the regular season, they went about their work like true professionals and that made the whole season a tremendous joy for all of the coaches.

'But the other thing,' added Criner, 'of equal importance, was to watch our crowds swell from last season. To see our fans learn about the game, adopt it, appreciate and understand it was tremendous. They knew how important it was to help our players on the field and they really did get behind them in the final. That's also a big part of why so many of our players want to come back. It's not just the winning, it's the people, too. Those two things mean more than lifting the trophy above my head – in fact, it's how we got to lift the trophy.'

It's an experience Jim Criner would like to repeat next season.

Murphy makes another acrobatic catch

THE AMERICAN PERSPECTIVE

Roddy McKenzie

18 April 1989. It was an unremarkable Tuesday in Scottish sport. A couple of days earlier, Celtic had beaten Hibernian at Hampden in the Scottish Football Association Cup semi-final to earn the right to face Rangers in the final. It was familiar stuff.

If Scottish sport was looking to new horizons, it was only because Scotland had been chosen to host the Under-16 World Cup at football a couple of months later. Little heed was paid to an announcement in New York that the NFL was to form a World League of American Football which would start in the spring of 1991.

It appeared of little concern to Scotland. There were a handful of amateur American football teams playing in the country but teams fell as quickly as they were established and media recognition was sparse. Yet on that Tuesday, the seeds of the Scottish Claymores were sown. The strategy was formed and the commitment received to pursue a league which included European teams.

Admittedly, Scotland was not on that original agenda. Instead, London, Frankfurt, Barcelona, Sacramento, Birmingham (Alabama), Montreal, Raleigh-Durham (North Carolina), Orlando, San Antonio and New York won the franchises in a ten-team league.

It was the latest attempt to globalise American football. Back in August 1976, the St Louis Cardinals defeated the San Diego Chargers 20–10 in Tokyo in the first NFL game to be played outside North America. In the next 14 years, exhibition matches featuring NFL teams – all healthily attended – were held in London, Mexico City, Gothenburg, Montreal, Tokyo and Berlin. NFL coaches and players were also making regular trips to Europe to spread the word.

Establishing a new league was a logical, if giant, step for the NFL. Two years down the line (after World Bowl wins for London Monarchs and Scaramento Surge), it was time for a rethink. At a meeting in Dallas on 17 September 1992, NFL clubs approved a proposal by the World League Board of Directors to restructure the league in a format that would include more European teams. Within a month, the European card had been firmly played. Oliver Luck, then general manager of Frankfurt Galaxy, opened the first NFL international office in Europe. Luck was also to oversee amateur development of the game.

However, it was in the autumn of 1993 that a new World League began to take shape. In Dallas in early September, NFL owners discussed an international business plan and then reconvened on 27 October when they approved a plan for a new six-team European league. By March of 1994, the NFL and Fox Inc. announced a joint partnership to back the new World League and stated that play would begin in 1995. London, Frankfurt and Barcelona were given three of the six available places. It was on 27 July at a news conference in London that Neil Austrian, the NFL president, finally confirmed the new league would open the following April and Amsterdam, Dusseldorf and Scotland would complete the line-up.

In 1996, average attendances in the World League increased by 20 per cent and, even before the World Bowl, the Claymores had boosted their attendance figures by just under 50 per cent. 'When you look back to where we started from, when we resurrected this league last year, you can see we have come a long way. Our average attendance has risen to over 17,000 and that compares well with all other sport in Europe,' says Neil Austrian.

'None of us believes we will overtake any of the traditional sports in Europe but we do believe there is a niche for our sport here. When you consider it is not a historic or cultural

Stacy runs headlong into the Galaxy defence

sport in Europe, the success of the World Bowl is a springboard for us next season. Broadcasting the World Bowl on Fox shows the maturity of the World League as well as our relationship with Fox Sports. It gave American fans a terrific chance to see what great players there are in Europe, many of whom could one day be playing for their local team.'

George Krieger, executive vice-president of Fox Sports, points out: 'Joining forces with the NFL in the World League was a logical expansion for us. Fox believes in American

football as a business, a live sports attraction and as a television property. We are going to continue moving forward and continue building a business with the NFL. Viewing figures are up across the board and have shown the growth and upward trend we anticipated. In 1996, we have added extensive US television coverage and have seen a 50 per cent increase in programming in Europe.'

Fox Sports underlined their commitment to the World League by using the World Bowl to jump-start their coverage of the 1996–97 NFL season which culminates in Super Bowl XXXI. They used their celebrated commentary team of Terry Bradshaw, Howie Long and James Brown to cover the action with play-by-play announcer Kevin Harlan and analyst Matt Millen to cover the World Bowl at Murrayfield.

Oliver Luck, the president of the World League, admits the Scottish Claymores have been one of the successes of the league. 'I've been delighted with what we have achieved in the past year. Scotland was a pleasant surprise for us with almost 39,000 turning up at Murrayfield for the World Bowl,' he states. 'It was hard to have any expectations after the Claymores' first season went so poorly but it has turned around completely with Jim Criner and Mike Keller and their staff doing a great job.

'There was a really big excitement about the game and, for us, it's all about trying to generate excitement in a new marketplace. American football is such a good spectator sport – you have the cheerleaders, the excitement of a match and the backfields party. People say it's a new sport in Europe but I liken it to boxing. Not a lot of people box any more but the crowds will come out to watch a boxing match when the big names are in town.'

He concedes there is still work to be done on the franchises but the upturn in attendances in 1996 showed that the World League is heading in the right direction. 'Nothing can happen overnight. What we have to have is patience – as long as we can see development in each of the outlets. In 1996, it was Scotland who were successful but next year it could be Amsterdam in their magnificent new stadium or Dusseldorf,' he points out.

What of the future? Luck admits that having only six teams is not the ideal situation and the proposal is to bring a further two teams on board in the 1998 season, though obviously costs will need to be scrutinised as there is a heavy financial outlay on creating a new team. 'Whether or not another two teams come on board will depend on how well the World League does next season. The NFL have also talked about extending it to Asia at some stage in the future but I do not know that market too well at present. To be honest, we have our hands full just working with Europe.

'I've only been to Japan once but the television ratings are good for the sport and there were over 40,000 fans at the American Bowl match in Tokyo this year, but it's too early to say at this stage whether Asia will be part of an expansion plan.'

So where does Luck see the World League in ten years' time? 'I'd like to see ten teams competing and maybe having two separate divisions – East and West or North and South – and having a true championship game at the end. I'd like to see every match played in front of the size of crowd we had at Murrayfield for this year's World Bowl. I'd also like to see the national players playing a bigger part.

'Every year in the World League we want to see the number of national players increase along with the quality of national players. It's all going to take time. I'm a former player myself and I know how hard it is to improve significantly in two or three years. I'd certainly like to see more players like Scott Couper emerging throughout Europe but it takes time for that to happen and these are long-term proposals.'

It seems the World League can never stand still and that goes for the teams involved. Ever conscious of this, Wil Wilson, the director of public relations for the Claymores, is always keen for the Scottish team to be ahead of the game. So it was, back in March 1996, even before a ball was kicked or thrown in the World League, the Scottish Claymores went global by setting up their own site on the Internet. It can be accessed at http://www.claymores.co.uk.

The site averaged 20,000 hits a week throughout the season from 40 countries throughout the world. The site is updated weekly with player/coach interviews, a cheerleaders page, merchandise updates, team records and such and, for next season, the Claymores are looking at using short video clips on the site to show key moments from matches.

The Claymores went on-line in late March and were the first World League team to have an official site on the Internet. Already it has won a national design award. 'The number of hits we received went up during the week's build-up to the World Bowl and there has been interest from all over the world. Our research shows that whereas 31 per cent of our calls are from Great Britain, 20 per cent are from the United States,' Wilson points out. 'The Internet is the future and we see it as a corner-piece in our communications jigsaw.'

The World League and the Scottish Claymores have given a new dimension to European sport. They will continue to explore new horizons into the next millennium.

Gordon Scott

There are ways of understanding why the Claymores are destined to become an established part of Scotland's sporting scene. The easiest is to listen to the optimistic proclamations of the men who turned the team from worst to first in 12 months.

Talk to head coach Jim Criner and he will tell you how the void left by the departure of Siran Stacy, the World League's most productive player, to pursue a career in the NFL, will be filled in 1997 by one of many top-rated targets. Meanwhile, marketing director John Hall will explain how the telephone he didn't think was working in 1995 is now ringing with calls from would-be sponsors before a ball is kicked. Above all, listen to Mike Keller, the team's general manager, who had the last laugh when his prediction of a 25,000 crowd for the World Bowl on 23 June – judged mere bravado by the cynics – turned into an actual attendance of nealry 40,000.

Alternatively, you could dodge the sabre-rattling and the marketing-speak and ask Shannon Wilson. Shannon is two years old, has a limited vocabulary and grins uncontrollably when large hairy monsters lurch towards her. More of her later.

For a true perspective, however, it is necessary to go back. Back to the future. Like some whizz-bang DeLorean sports car, the Claymores machine landed in Scotland in September 1994 with much excitement, expectation and not a little spark-flying. The locals were wary. Football, established for more than a century, ruled the roost. The message was clear: tinkering with the course of history doesn't work. Just ask Michael J. Fox.

Perhaps if the Claymores had provided a winning team, things would have been different. Sadly, early indications that the team could play a bit proved unfounded. Two victories from ten, neither of them at Murrayfield, prompted mediocre attendances and sceptical coverage from a largely xenophobic press corps.

The funny thing was, everyone still knew who the Scottish Claymores were. And that was a start. 'Oh, there was an awareness of the team all right,' said Keller. 'Although I would have preferred if the awareness had been a little more positive.' They were, in the eyes of all but the most die-hard American football fans, a laughing stock. That the Scottish Claymores have turned that image around is the most compelling evidence that the future is bright. There were, of course, equally compelling excuses for the initial failure, not least the fact that the team's Scottish office opened in October and the team was assembled on paper in January for a training camp in March, with a view to their first game in April.

The establishment of the organisation always meant the second year would be different. Lessons were learned about how to deal with the business community and the team's landlords at the headquarters of the Scottish Rugby Union. There was time to understand the simple geography of their adoptive country which made it possible to house the players, and adopt a new training facility in Glasgow. The behind-the-scenes staff climbed the learning curve and attacked the problems of the first season with gusto and the confidence that comes from understanding the environment.

In stark contrast, the team itself, which actually had something to shout about, having ended the previous season with a morale-boosting victory against the Monarchs in London, played it cool. The hype of 1995 had subsided.

Those of us fortunate enough to attend the eight post-victory press conferences at home and abroad in the season just past recall how coach Criner opened every briefing with a cry of 'How 'Bout them Claymores!'. But that was about it in the shout-it-from-the-rooftops stakes. Somebody had told the team that situations where words and action are in inverse proportion to each other have not gone down well in Scotland since the time the nation's soccer stars travelled to Argentina in 1978, pledging, under the extrovert leadership of Ally MacLeod, to win the World Cup and, to cut a long story short, didn't.

In 1996, the approach was altogether more cautious, from the moment the Claymores started winning at the training camp in Atlanta. Explained Keller: 'Looking back to 1995, the team won a few practice matches in Atlanta and started shooting their mouths off, creating a perception that Scotland had the best team in the league. The team played to win all their scrimmage matches, while the opposition didn't show their hands. The result was that people back home in Scotland were misled. When the Claymores started playing for real in Europe – and started losing – the public felt cheated.' They were not the only ones.

Lodged for three months, two to a room, in an isolated hotel on the outskirts of Edinburgh, the players became increasingly disillusioned. One source has since admitted: 'Basically, the players were not prepared to do the necessary to win.' This season has been different and the Claymores will be based in Glasgow again in 1997.

No team has ever successfully defended the World Bowl but the recent confirmation that Criner and his team of coaches will return for next season has ensured continuity of leadership and ideas. Among the players, all but Stacy have confirmed that they, too, if required, will be back. News that former Claymores quarterback Steve Matthews, one of nearly 20 former Claymores in the ranks of the NFL, kicked off the season for the Kansas City Chiefs with 123 passing yards, suggests that many may indeed have other commitments.

However, Criner, a world-class fly fisherman, has an enviable reputation for his ability to lure players to his cause. If he could persuade one former Super Bowl winner, Jason Buck, to fly to Scotland at two days' notice on the strength of one call to the defenceman's mobile telephone in the middle of his Utah ranch, fans should not worry about the quality of next season's recruits. While all this was going on, John Hall's telephone was also ringing. Sponsorship increased by 300 per cent to £135,000 last season, from a broad base of companies keen to be associated with a family sport – and Gavin Hastings.

There is no disputing the impact of the G-force in driving the Claymores to new heights. While Scots-born Canadian Paul McCallum is a fine kicker – and how the team needed him in 1995 – he alone could not have sold the extra 2,000 tickets per match Hastings's presence has been estimated to have accounted for. Nor could McCallum have bridged the gaps between the Claymores and a business community indifferent to their sport, or indeed a somewhat reluctant Scottish Rugby Union. Keller refers to Hastings as a 'sports icon'; team-mates spoke of the former Scotland rugby captain in the same terms as Michael Jordan and Joe Montana. Hastings has yet to decide what his role in 1997 will be, though his sports management company is likely to be heavily involved.

'I have to admit that the signing of Gavin Hastings had some influence on our decision to become involved with the Claymores,' said Paul Yole, Kwik-Fit's marketing director. 'It showed us that the club meant business for the season; that they were thinking big. But that on its own was never enough. What the Claymores achieved last year, both with their performances on the field and the family entertainment they provided, has built a platform for the future. The weather was lousy, but people kept coming back.'

Zeno and Ballard ready to start the play

With or without Hastings on the field, Yole believes sponsors will return. He added: 'Because of what they have done in the past and what they are planning for the future, the Claymores have the opportunity to secure some very valuable sponsors. They have arrived as a marketing force.'

A measure of the organisation's ambition lies with the fact that rumours that the Rolling Stones were to be invited to provide the entertainment at the backfields party prior to the World Bowl were almost unbelievable. In the end, Abba and U2 soundalike bands did enough early in the season to convince the public of the quality of the pre-match entertainment. For every ten people who attended a game for the first time, eight returned. Better bands are planned for 1997 with a bigger, slicker presentation. It has been suggested that the in-stadium video screen will display explanations of some of the more complex refereeing decisions.

Moves to personalise the heavily padded and face-masked players, and to promote the

Claymores cheerleaders with mascot Shuggie

fact that they are among the élite in a sport that has only 2,000 professional players world-wide, may also be forthcoming.

Some of the personalities need no further introductions, however, and the real hope for the future is reflected in the eyes of Shannon Wilson. At the age of two years, Shannon was a second-season veteran of Claymores games. Her smiling face filled the giant television screen during the World Bowl as the roving reporter interviewed three generations of the Wilson family. Though her vocabulary may have subsequently improved, Shannon's part in the dialogue that day consisted of just one word: 'Shuggie'.

The object of her desire is the most unlikely of sporting heroes. A great gallumphing cuddly bear, Shuggie is the Claymores' kilt-wearing, bug-eyed mascot. Quite frankly, Shannon, like many people in the crowd, didn't know what the Claymores' West Coast Offence was all about and cared that Gavin Hastings missed the odd kick even less. However, when Shuggie ambled towards her, Shannon's eyes lit up and her parents knew why they had taken her to Murryafield.

'Let's face it,' said another parent during the course of the season. 'It was great when the Claymores won but it didn't exactly ruin the rest of our week when they lost. Can the football fans who go to watch Hearts, Hibs, Rangers or whoever say that? We took the kids and we ALL had great fun.'

There is another reason to be hopeful that the Scottish Claymores are here for the long haul. For, that most American of sports, played amid the love-it-or-hate-it excesses of transatlantic razzmatazz, has been given a vote of confidence by one of Scotland's most established, and outwardly conservative, companies. It took five meetings and a considerable amount of negotiation to convince Kinloch Anderson that producing a Claymores tartan was not a short-term gimmick, reservations perhaps that summed up a whole nation's initial caution. Now, when Mike Keller wears his blue and silver Claymores kilt, he remembers two battles won – over Frankfurt Galaxy and over the Scottish public. 'Listen,' he says proudly. 'It was the kilt shop people who persuaded us to put mini-kilts on the cheerleaders.'

The Scottish Claymores, all sweat, sequins and tartan, is a partnership built to last.

Steve Livingstone

To the uninitiated, watching gridiron for the first time can seem a little daunting – if not downright confusing – but the concept of the American game is surprisingly straightforward. Indeed, it developed from the basic principles of rugby football and soccer introduced to North America by Europeans.

THE HISTORY

When the British and Europeans settled in America and Canada at the start of the nineteenth century, they brought their games with them. Indeed, the first development of what we know today as gridiron has its origins in a soccer-like game which was played at the universities of north-east America – colleges such as Yale, Harvard and Princeton. The last gave its name to the first set of American football rules, which were drawn up in 1867. Two years later, on 6 November 1869, the first intercollegiate game took place in New Brunswick, New Jersey, where Rutgers college defeated Princeton 6–4 on a field with makeshift goalposts whose uprights were 25 yards apart. In a return match the following week Princeton won 8–0.

At its inception the game was predominantly a kicking event, but at Harvard new rules were developed which introduced running with the ball as in rugby. No one else in the north-east was keen on adopting the Harvard rules, known to historians as 'The Boston Game', so a Canadian rugby team from McGill University in Montreal was invited to travel the 250 miles to Cambridge, Massachusetts, to play Harvard under the new code. Unfortunately, four members of the McGill team fell ill before making the journey leaving the match to go ahead on 15 May 1874 with 11 instead of the usual 15 players.

The game, complete with proper goalposts, proved an enormous success and slowly the other 'Ivy League' colleges took up the same style of play. In 1875 Harvard played Yale in the first game between two American colleges under the new rules. A year later five colleges met to form the Intercollegiate Football Association, based on the code and ethics of rugby. The rugby style of heeling the ball back from a scrummage was used until 1880 when Walter Camp, the father of the modern game, introduced the 'scrimmage' and a grid of lines on the field – hence the name gridiron – in an attempt to develop a 'more orderly game'.

The improbably named Amos Alonzo Stagg was next to make a huge impact on the developing sport introducing the huddle in 1894. Stagg, a great coach and innovator, also added refinements to the game which included the centre snap; man in motion; reverses, diagrammed play books, backfield shifts, tackling dummies and numbers on shirts. By 1912 American football had developed its present form and the first superstar of the sport – native American and Olympic gold medallist Jim Thorpe – put the professional game on the map. In 1925 football fever gripped America when George Halas's Chicago Bears, featuring the legendary Red Grange, criss-crossed America on a barnstorming tour, playing 19 games in 66 days.

The tour had been made possible by a meeting held in a garage in Canton, Ohio, five years earlier, where the formation of a professional league – the American Professional Football Association (APFA) – was discussed by the owners of ten teams who sat on the running boards of eight cars in the garage showroom. By 1922 the APFA was known as the National Football League (NFL) – the forerunner to American football's professional governing body of today, out of which the World League of American Football (WLAF) was developed.

THE FUNDAMENTALS

During the Green Bay Packers' offensive slump of the 1960s, legendary head coach Vince Lombardi called a team meeting. 'We're going to get back to basics,' said Lombardi. 'Back to the fundamentals. Now this,' he said, holding up a ball, 'is a football.'

'Hold on, coach,' interrupted wide receiver Max McGhee. 'You're going too fast.'

McGhee proved it doesn't do any harm to go on a refresher course whether you're playing or just watching. In fact, watching the game for the first time can seem a little complex and confusing. However, the concept of the game is relatively simple: it's about territory and position where both teams on the field have one aim – to score more points than the other by running or passing the ball across the opponents' goal line, or by kicking it through the opponents' goalposts.

THE BALL

Lombardi was right when he stressed to his Packers that the football is the most fundamental feature of the game. It not only gives the sport its name, but its unusual shape also makes the action of the game quite unique.

The official football used in the World League and NFL is a rubber bladder inflated to 12.5 to 13.5 psi, enclosed in a pebble-grained casting of natural tan-coloured leather – not, as is the popular myth, pigskin – weighing 14 to 15 ounces.

THE FIELD

Types of surfaces in the NFL vary from stadium to stadium, but in the World League all six teams play outdoors on natural grass. The other constant throughout the league is the shape, size and markings on the field. A World League football field is rectangular in shape measuring 120 yards long by 53⅓ yards wide. The actual field of play is 100 yards long, with two ten-yard deep sections called **endzones** extending from each goal line.

Parallel to the goal line, the field is sectioned off every five yards with **yard lines**. These are numbered every ten yards up to the 50-yard line, or **midfield stripe**, and give the field its distinctive **gridiron** look. A pair of parallel dotted lines, called **hashmarks**, run from goal line to goal line and down the centre of the field defining an area within which the ball is placed after every down. The hashmarks are one yard apart with the two lines 18.5 feet apart. This is the same space as the distance between the **uprights** on each of the two goalposts.

One line you won't see marked in football though, is the **line of scrimmage**. This is an imaginary line parallel to the goal line determined by where the ball is placed or **spotted** after a play ends. On each play, the offensive and defensive teams line up on either side of it. Between the two teams is a **neutral zone** which measures the length of the ball. Neither team may enter this area before the ball is **snapped**. This area is also known as **The Trenches**.

THE PLAYERS

A full American football squad is actually made up of three separate units: the **offence**, the **defence** and the **special teams unit**. Ordinarily, during the course of a game, it's the offence's job to score points, the defence's to prevent the opponent from scoring and the special teams' to obtain good field position for its offence or defence or to score itself with the field goal.

Only **11 players** – thanks to the cut down McGill University touring squad – are allowed on the field at any one time, although each of the three units on a squad will have up to three or four substitutes and specialists adding to a full team of around 42 players. Each player is assigned a specific **position** on his unit, although special teams' players usually also play on either the offence or defence.

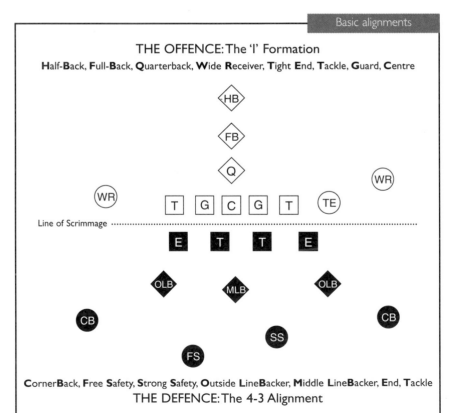

Basic alignments

THE OFFENCE: The 'I' Formation
Half-**B**ack, **F**ull-**B**ack, **Q**uarterback, **W**ide **R**eceiver, **T**ight **E**nd, **T**ackle, **G**uard, **C**entre

Line of Scrimmage

Corner**B**ack, **F**ree **S**afety, **S**trong **S**afety, **O**utside **L**ine**B**acker, **M**iddle **L**ine**B**acker, **E**nd, **T**ackle
THE DEFENCE: The 4-3 Alignment

The starting offensive team usually consists of:
• Offensive line (blockers) – made up of the centre, two tackles and two guards.
• Receivers – usually two wide receivers and a tight end. However, any combination – three receivers, two tight ends, etc. – can be used.
• The backfield – including the quarterback and his running backs – a full-back and half-back, who are also eligible to catch the ball.

The defence also consists of three groups of players:

• Defensive line – three, four or even five players who attack the run or pass.
• Linebackers – three or four depending on formation who read and react.
• Defensive secondary – usually consisting of two cornerbacks and two safeties, strong and free, who primarily defend against the pass.

Besides a **head coach**, each team also has a staff of **assistant coaches**. Their numbers vary with each team and each specialises in working with certain positions – such as receivers, the offensive line, linebackers – or on areas of strategy, such as co-ordinating the offensive or defensive plays.

• World League teams consist of a 42-man roster plus four-man practice squads made up of:
34 … Active players
7 … National players
1 … Inactive, third quarterback
• Each team is required to contain seven national players on its roster for the entire season. All seven national players must be active for every game and must play in 50 per cent of all downs.

GAINING YARDAGE AND POSSESSION

Progress on the football field is measured in **yards**. The team in **possession** of the ball, on offence, has four chances or **downs**, to move the ball ten yards. The offence will do this by running a series of set-piece moves called **plays**. If a team can achieve its ten-yard objective within its allotted four downs, it is allowed to retain possession – called **gaining a first down** – and is given a new set of downs to continue driving downfield.

For instance, if Claymores running back Siran Stacy makes four yards on a first down, that would bring up a second-and-six play. If quarterback Jim Ballard then threw a three-yard pass to receiver Scott Couper the Claymores would be left facing a third down and three. If

FACT BOX: TEAM PERSONNEL

All World League players are numbered according to their positions, while each team is made up of a certain number of players at each of the positions.

POSITION NUMBERING:
1–19 Quarterbacks and kickers
20–49 Running backs and defensive backs
50–59 Centres and linebackers
60–79 Defensive linemen and interior offensive linemen
80–89 Wide receivers and tight ends
90–99 Defensive linemen

NUMBERS IN POSITIONS:

Offensive linemen	8
Receivers	6
Running backs	5
Quarterbacks	3
Defensive linemen	6
Linebackers	6
Defensive backs	6
Kicker	1
Punter	1
TOTAL	42

Stacy then ran more than three yards on the Claymores next play the Scots would be awarded a first down, with the **down markers** on the sideline moving towards the opposition goal line to signpost the next ten-yard objective.

Down and distance are carefully measured by two officials called linesmen, who head up the **chain gang** stationed along the sideline. If the offence fails to make a first down, and is not within field goal range, the **punting team** will be sent on, usually on fourth down, to **punt** the ball as far downfield as possible in an attempt to start the opponent's offence deep in their own territory. In World League rules the defence is allowed to rush only three players per side of the ball on punts. If the offence tries to make a first down and fails on fourth down their opponent gets the ball and a first down where the play fell short.

MOVING THE BALL

Once the offence gains possession of the ball, they have several options for gaining yardage to advance the ball and score points. Prior to the play the quarterback will marshall his unit in the **huddle** to discuss the best plan of attack, and with advice from the coaching staff – via the headset in his helmet or signals from the sideline – will **call the play**.

A 'handoff' play

Running

Technically, any offensive player can run the ball, but it's almost always the running backs who take on this role. Wide receivers, tight ends and even quarterbacks on a play called a **bootleg** can carry the ball. But QBs usually only run with it on **short yardage situations** or when forced to **scramble** by defenders on a pass rush.

The most basic running play is the **handoff**, where the quarterback takes the **snap** from the centre, turns and places the ball into the hands of the running back who is rushing towards the line of scrimmage and behind the **run blocking** of his offensive line. On some plays the quarterback will **fake** the handoff to one runner and then handoff to the other. The QB may also fake the handoff before dropping back to pass, called **play-action**.

A variation of the handoff is the **pitchout** or **toss**. Here, the QB turns from the snap to make an underhand toss to one of his running backs sweeping wide to one side of the field. This type of running play is typically known as a **sweep** and the runner may have the added luxury of a pulling lineman who rolls out from the offensive line to block for him.

Passing

Although a team's quarterback does most of the passing, legally any offensive player can do so. After taking the snap, the quarterback drops back into the **pocket**, a semi-circle of protection provided by his offensive line, who **pass block** to form the pocket. As he drops, the quarterback will read the defence and scan the field attempting to find an open receiver. The quarterback usually has to do this under pressure from the **pass rush**, as defensive linemen go all out to attack him. If a defender tackles the quarterback behind the line of scrimmage before he can throw the ball he is said to have made a **sack**.

The only offensive players who are not eligible to catch passes are the five interior linemen (centre, tackles and guards). Passes can be caught anywhere within the field of play. In the World League, for a pass to be ruled a **completion**, the receiver must have the ball clearly in his possession and have one foot inside the boundaries of either the sidelines or endzone. In the NFL, two feet are required to stay in bounds or the catch will be ruled an incompletion, out of bounds.

There are 11 more eligible receivers the quarterback does his best to avoid: the defence. Anyone on the defence can intercept the passer. Any **interception** has the potential to be returned for a touchdown. Because both receivers and defenders have equal right to catch the ball, neither is allowed to impede the other from doing so. If this happens, the officials will rule **pass interference** on the guilty party. Defensive pass interference in the World League carries a hefty penalty, where the offence is given an automatic first down at the point of the interference, unless it is unintentional, where a 15-yard penalty from the line of scrimmage is enforced. Offensive pass interference carries a ten-yard penalty and loss of down.

Quarterback drops back into the 'pocket'

A team in possession is allowed to make **one forward pass** which must be thrown from behind the line of scrimmage, although an unlimited number of **lateral** passes are allowed on any play behind or beyond the line. A lateral must be passed to a team-mate who is alongside or behind the passer.

TURNOVERS

Punting is not the only way of handing possession to the opponent, or **turning the ball over** on downs. Forced turnovers occur out of mistakes on the offence. **Fumbling** possession away, when a ball carrier drops the ball to be recovered by the other team, or throwing the **interception**, results in a turnover and can be advanced by the defence.

PENALTIES

The ball can be advanced or brought back by means of the **penalty** assessed by the officials. Penalties usually range from five to 15 yards and/or a loss of down, depending on the infraction and the situation where and when it takes place. When a penalty is assessed, one or more of the seven officials on the field throws a yellow marker, called a **flag**.

There are **seven officials** on the field, led by the referee who has general control of the game and final authority on rules' interpretations. The other officials include the umpire, head linesman, line judge, back judge, field judge and side judge.

SCORING POINTS

There are five ways to score points in the World League (only four in the NFL).

A **touchdown**, worth **six points**, is awarded when a player **breaks the plane** of the opponents' goal line with the football. This can be done by running the ball into the endzone OR by catching the ball in the endzone OR by recovering an opponent's fumble in the endzone.

Following a touchdown, the scoring team is given a chance to score either **one** or **two extra points** with the ball placed at the two-yard line for a **conversion** attempt. A kicked conversion through the uprights is worth one point, however, the head coach can elect to opt for a two-point conversion where the ball once again has to break the plane of the goal line via the run or pass. The two-pointer becomes important in close games or when a team has to come back from a points deficit.

On any one of its four downs the offence can attempt a kick at goal worth **three points**. The **field goal** is roughly the equivalent to a penalty goal in rugby, however, it will normally be attempted on fourth down when the offence is within good field goal range – between ten and 40 yards.

An attempted 'field goal'

A kick is measured from the yardage position on the field, plus the distance between the goal line and uprights (ten yards from the front of the endzone), plus the distance between the line of scrimmage and the point the ball is spotted by the holder for the kicker (usually around seven yards). Therefore, a kick attempted from the 20-yard line, if successful, will actually measure a 37-yard field goal. In the World League a field goal measuring **50 or more yards** is awarded **four points**.

The defence can score touchdowns but also has a unique way of adding points to the scoreboard with a **safety**. A safety, worth **two points**, is scored when a defender tackles any member of the offence caught in possession, carrying or holding the ball in his own endzone. A safety is also scored if the ball carrier runs, or is forced to run, through the back of his own endzone or if the ball is snapped or fumbled over the endline. The two-pointer can also be awarded by the officials if an offensive player is ruled guilty of a holding or similar violation while in the endzone.

Finally, unique to the World League, is the **deuce**, also worth **two points**. A deuce is scored when the defence runs back a blocked point after a touchdown kick or intercepted two-point pass attempt into the opponents' endzone.

TIMING

While the actual **game clock** in a World League football game ticks down 60 minutes, the match usually lasts around two and a half hours. This is because the game clock is not continuous and can be stopped in a number of ways.

The game is divided into four periods of **15 minutes**, called **quarters**, separated by a 15-minute half-time break between the second and third quarters. To ensure an equal experience of weather and playing conditions the teams change ends after every quarter. The first and third quarters begin with a kick-off. The kick-off also restarts play after a touchdown or field goal is scored. Following a safety, a free kick from the 20-yard line is taken to restart the game. In addition to the quarter and half-time breaks, each team is permitted to call three 90-second **time-outs** during each half. The game clock is stopped during time-outs.

The game clock also stops when the ball goes **out of bounds** or when a pass is thrown **incomplete**. Officials can also call time-outs to assess penalties, measure yardage, replace equipment, tend to injured players and to inform both sets of coaches on the sidelines that two minutes remain in the second and fourth quarters, called the **two-minute warning**.

The offence must deal with an additional time limit between plays – **the 35-second play clock**. Unless each offensive play begins within 35 seconds of the referee's whistle indicating that the ball has been spotted and play is ready to resume, the offensive team is penalised with a **delay of game** penalty where the ball is moved back five yards.

If a match is tied after four quarters the game goes into a ten-minute **overtime**. In the World League each team must have one possession before the overtime period goes into **sudden death**, when the first team to score wins the match.

PLAYS AND TACTICS

While understanding a little of the strategy and tactics of the game won't turn you into the next Jim Criner, it will enhance your enjoyment of what you are watching the next time you go to Murrayfield during the World League season. This section is intended as an introduction to some of the most popular and enduring of football tactics as well as a look at those successful strategies and plays used by Scottish Claymores head coach Jim Criner and his coaching staff in their pursuit of World Bowl glory.

Running the ball successfully in football is crucial to any team's success. Without establishing a solid running attack any offence will find it difficult to implement their passing game. However, running the ball well requires more than just having a great rusher like Siran Stacy on your team. The key to successful running is good **run blocking** – moving defenders out of the way to stop them from getting to your ball carrier.

The most basic type of line blocking is the traditional **power**, **drive** or **straight-ahead** block. However, offensive linemen use a variety of blocks and combinations of blocks alone or as part of a double team to control the defender in front and to open up **running lanes** for the ball carrier.

Formation	Description
WR □□■□□ TE WR Q FB HB	**I Formation:** A basic run formation where both running backs line up behind the quarterback.
WR □□■□□ TE WR Q HB FB	**Split (Pro) Formation:** Here the running backs are split to either side of the quarterback, allowing the offence to pass more easily.
WR □□■□□ TE WR HB Q FB	**Double Wing Formation:** Better Receiver of two running backs lines up outside tackle to get free on pass.
WR □□■□□ TE WR HB Q FB	**Spread Formation:** Split backs outside the tackles allowing five receivers to be available.
TE □□■□□ WR Q FB WR HB (slot)	**Slot Formation:** Both receivers line up on one side, the tight end on the other with the running backs in any formation behind.
WR □□■□□ WR WR HB FB Q	**Shotgun Formation:** Similar to spread, except that the quarterback lines up for long snap five to seven yards behind the centre.
WR □□■□□ TE WR Q HB FB	**Opposite/Far Formation (Brown):** Full-back behind the quarterback and half-back on weakside allows easy run to that side.
WR □□■□□ TE WR Q HB FB	**Near Formation (Blue):** Similar to far but run to strongside with extra blocking power from the tight end.

Basic offensive formations

TYPES OF RUN PLAY

Running directed up the middle in the area between the guards is generally called **inside running**. Offences who control the the ball and the clock are particularly good in this area. Inside running is sometimes referred to as **mud-and-guts** football – seen on the **dive** play to the full-back – gaining short yardage and first downs the hard way.

Running inside can also be accomplished with the **lead** play where the full-back blocks a path for the half-back up through a specified hole in the line. The various holes or gaps on the offensive line are usually numbered between zero and nine, with the holes on the left numbered odd and the holes on the right numbered even. Hence the strange coded play-calling that is so often associated with gridiron. A typical run play would hear the quarterback in the huddle calling 'I, right, 34, lead' where, from the I formation, with the tight end on the right, the half-back (3) would carry the ball behind the full-back (who leads) up through the four hole on the right side of the line between the guard and tackle.

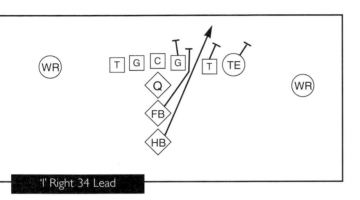

'I' Right 34 Lead

Running outside is characterised by two of the most basic plays in football: the **off-tackle** and the **sweep**.

The off-tackle consists of a simple handoff to the running back, who angles his run outside of either the left or right offensive tackle and inside the tight end. Because of the extra blocking potential of the tight end, defences are compelled to line a linebacker in front of the tight end (known as the **strong side** or SAM linebacker). However, if the offence can consistently find holes on the off-tackle play, the defence will be forced to bolster the strong side, perhaps even bringing one of the safeties to defend it, thus weakening the middle and the **weakside** (usually the side without tight end) of the defence.

The sweep takes the off-tackle a step further, going around the corner of the offensive line rather than through the edge. It's aimed to go outside the tight end and the strongside linebacker and towards the defensive back.

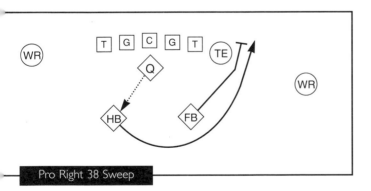

Pro Right 38 Sweep

Offensive linemen have to be quick on the sweep with the guards usually having the responsibilty of pulling out from their position to the outside to block for the running back. There are three types of sweep: the **power sweep**, which has both guards pulling to lead block for the runner; the **full-back sweep**, which sees the full-back block for the half-back; and the **option sweep**, which can involve the quarterback pulling out with the option of pitching to the running back, or the

running back pulling out with the option of passing the ball downfield to a receiver.

Much of the yardage Siran Stacy enjoyed this season was gained using a combination of these two plays, either running the sweep or off-tackle. Stacy followed his blockers but, in many instances, read the way the defenders reacted and managed to exploit outside lanes by **bouncing-out** from the off-tackle play or inside to open gaps by **cutting back** from the sweep if his opponents reacted well to the planned play.

Another mainstay of coach Criner's running game was the power sweep where Stacy kicked off the block provided by tight end Willy Tate or huge pulling guard Purvis Hunt.

Stacy follows blocker's lead

Claymores' power sweep

Pro Right 38
Power Sweep

THE AIR ATTACK

Running is one way to gain ground. Potentially much more spectacular is the **passing game**. While the Claymores were successful with a balanced offensive attack last season, it was their receivers in Kansas City Chiefs allocate Sean LaChapelle, Glaswegian Scott Couper and World Bowl MVP Yo Murphy who grabbed all the newspaper headlines.

However, yet again the success of any passing offence can be measured against how effective its **pass blocking** is – vital not only to protect the quarterback in the **pass pocket** but also to give receivers time to get open downfield on their **pass routes**. Offensive co-ordinator Jim Sochor installed a **West Coast** style offence during the Claymores' championship season which employed both short and deep passing routes to great effect. **Motion** and **play-action** were its staples, used to confuse opposing defences. **Timing**, **quick reads** and **execution** were its keys as the Scots' passing attack, ranked second in the

World League and directed first of all by quarterback Steve Matthews and then by Jim Ballard, notched up 2,210 yards (a 221 per game average) through the air in the regular season.

The Pass Masters

In receivers LaChapelle, Murphy and Couper, the Claymores had three of the best in the league. Added to their contribution, wideout Lee Gissendaner and tight end Willy Tate also made the grade reaping the rewards of hours spent running routes on the Claymores practice field under the direction of young receivers coach Vince Alcalde.

Fakes, cuts and precision were perfected there along with the timing crucial to the success of Sochor's scheme – and it paid dividends throughout the season, but especially as the Claymores booked their World Bowl ticket in Frankfurt with LaChapelle's perfectly executed and now famous 92-pass route which broke the deadlock and downed German champions Frankfurt.

It was a play LaChapelle

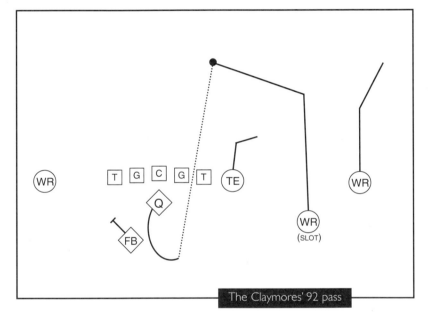

Yo Murphy after scoring a Claymores touchdown

The Claymores' 92 pass

had run thousands of times in practice and one which exemplified the effectiveness of a well-executed pass route – a short play which took advantage of a defensive weakness, splitting its secondary in two for a huge gain.

Sochor's short passing game was a joy to watch with **delay patterns**, **screen passes**, **flare passes**, **quick passes** to the tight end, **pick plays** and **underneath** routes all used. All of the Claymores receivers were capable of making yardage after the catch, too – with some of the most spectacular plays coming this way. Think back to LaChapelle's devastating sideline receptions in Frankfurt or Murphy's stunning **hook and go** for a 71-yard touchdown roared on by the massive Murrayfield World Bowl crowd.

The **long passing** game was also effective – the quickest way to get six on the board, as Scott Couper proved, catching Jim Ballard's 36-yard bomb in Barcelona. The objective of the long passing game is to isolate one or more receivers downfield against just one defender deep. Couper turned that theory on its head, the single receiver catching in double coverage, just as LaChapelle had shown six weeks earlier against Rhein Fire.

One of the most popular methods of keeping the defence off balance is to use the **play-action** pass and with Siran Stacy, Ron Dickerson and Jared Kaaiohelo in the backfield it was more easy yardage for the Claymores' passing attack last season. But perhaps the most successful short pass was the **screen** to Stacy behind the awesome line blocking of Purvis Hunt, Keith Wagner, Tom Barndt, Matt Storm, Randy Bierman and Lance Zeno in any combination, depending on which side the play was run.

One of the advantages of running the screen, which provides a wall of blockers for the running back who makes the catch behind the line of scrimmage, was the additional running room it created for Stacy behind that wall of solid blocking.

DEFENCE WINS CHAMPIONSHIPS

The age-old gridiron cliché was proved yet again last season as defensive guru Ray Willsey's defence played a huge role in bringing the World Bowl to Scotland. Defensive tactics can be complicated but it all boiled down to one basic idea summed up by Willsey: 'I like a defence that hits and gets after people. I call it the run and hit defence.'

If the offence's main weapon is surprise, the defence has to be sure to cover every possible angle and to be able to **read** or **key** the offence.

The Claymores' defensive line

THE 4–3 DEFENCE

While the latest trend in the NFL is away from the 3–4 (three down linemen and four linebackers) defence in adoption of the 4–3 (two **defensive tackles**, two **defensive ends** and three **linebackers**) set-up, Willsey already had his in place when he took on the job of Claymores defensive co-ordinator last March.

Bringing a heavier presence to the line than the 3–4, the 4–3 was the primary defence used in the NFL through the '50s and '60s. The 4–3, with its extra defensive lineman, works well against the run with more tacklers waiting for the running back at the line of scrimmage, the idea being that four defensive front men can better neutralise the blocks of five offensive linemen than three can. For the same reason – one more lineman – defences using the 4–3 can generate a much greater **pass rush**.

However, the onus is shifted to the **linebackers**. Three linebackers – typically labelled **Sam**, **Mac** and **Will** (strongside, middle and weakside) – position themselves behind the defensive line with the Mac backer placing himself anywhere between the defensive tackles, with the outside backers flexible to align themselves inside or outside of the ends, depending on the situation (see basic alignment graphic).

All three linebackers in the 4–3 must be extremely mobile, as they are responsible for **covering** a greater area than the four backers in the 3–4. To compensate for their large territories, and to confuse the quarterback, the linebackers will frequently adjust their position and alignment, constantly moving around to new areas to support the down linemen and fill expected running lanes.

GETTING IT COVERED

Behind the linebackers, occupying the **defensive secondary** are two **cornerbacks**, a **strong** and a **free safety**. Typically dubbed the last line of defence, it's the secondary's role not only primarily to defend against the pass but also to assist in stopping the run.

Defending against the pass was something the Claymores secondary did extremely well last season with safeties George Coghill, James Fuller and David Wilson leading the league in interceptions. However, the Claymores defensive backs also had a reputation as **hard hitters** able to bring their own brand of stopping power to defend against the run.

Generally, three different types of defence or **coverage** are employed against the pass. While the defensive line tries to put pressure on the quarterback with a **pass rush** the linebackers and defensive backs can slip into various coverages which include:

• **Man-to-man**: where each player on the defence marks or covers a particular player on the offence. **Bump and run**, a form of man coverage where the defender bumps the receiver at the line of scrimmage before trailing him downfield, is also popular in a bid to put the receiver out of stride.

• **Zone coverage**: where instead of marking a man the defender will be responsible for covering an area or zone of the field. In a 4–3 defence the field is usually divided into seven zones, **shallow** and **deep**. One of the first zone defences was devised by legendary Green Bay Packers head coach Vince Lombardi.

• **Combination** (man and zone): where some defenders will cover a specific receiver while others will guard an area or zone of the field.

In adopting these coverages the defensive co-ordinator may also increase the number of

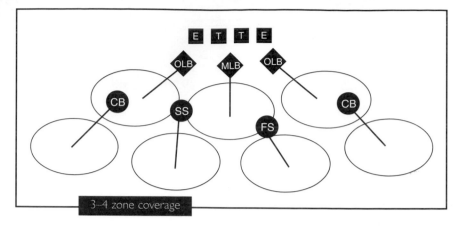

3–4 zone coverage

defensive backs at the expense of less agile linebackers to provide greater protection down-field. This is particularly prevalent in surefire passing situations, or perhaps when an opponent just likes to pass the ball deep.

A formation with five defensive backs is known as a **nickel** defence. A formation with six defensive backs is called a **dime** defence.

DOGGING AND BLITZING

While defences rely on the line to attack the quarterback in passing situations, even more pressure can be put on the passer if the defensive co-ordinator decides to gamble on increasing the number of his defenders rushing the passer.

Dogging and blitzing sends not only linemen after the quarterback but also linebackers and defensive backs – but at the expense of full pass coverage downfield. The saying '*live by the blitz, die by the blitz*' was coined for teams who risk too much and leave themselves open by rushing too many defenders. However, the rewards for pressuring or getting to the quarterback are potentially greater with the prospect of a momentum-shifting sack or interception.

In a **dog** a linebacker (or any combination of linebackers) leaves his regular area of coverage to join the pass rush on an immediate or delayed attack. A **blitz** involves a cornerback or safety, or any combination of defensive backs, rushing the passer. Whereas a dog can be used to stop the run as well as the pass, the blitz is used primarily to stop only the pass, although it leaves the defence vulnerable to the quick pass or run.

Defensive co-ordinator Ray Willsey liked to gamble with dogs and blitzes throughout the Claymores' season, with one of the most memorable blitzes coming in the week-five win over Frankfurt Galaxy when cornerback James Williams streaked upfield, taking Galaxy quarterback Brad Bretz completely by surprise to record his first sack on a corner blitz.

THE SPECIAL-TEAMERS

The special teams squads are as important as both the offence and the defence, as **the kicking game** accounts for one-third of play and more importantly, is the key to unlocking good field position to make the defence's and offence's jobs easier.

Modern American football strategy relies heavily on the special teams, which can be divided into six distinct areas. Special teams include the **kick-off** team, the **kick-off return**, the **punt team**, the **punt return**, the **field goal** and the **extra point**. The reason they are so important is that in nearly every kicking situation there is the possibility of a touchdown being scored on both sides of the ball.

The kick-off

On a kick-off the ball is placed on the kicking team's **35-yard line**. The aim is to kick the ball as deep as possible while limiting the returner to as short a return as possible. Members of the kick-off unit are assigned positions along a line to the left and right of the kicker, with the fastest **cover men** placed near the sideline to contain the returner, and the bigger and **harder hitters** aligned nearer the middle, to deal with blocks and make the tackles.

Aggressiveness is also required down the middle to break through any **return wedge** that may have been set up. Discipline is also important because kick-off coverage men must stay in their **lanes** to cover the field before converging on the returner.

The **onside kick** is a short kick used to regain possession in crucial situations. On kick-offs the ball is considered live and can be recovered by the kick team

Hastings prepares for the 'kick-off'

after it has gone ten yards. However, the onside kick is a risky strategy and is only usually employed in last-ditch situations when a team needs to score to save or win a match. Coaches will usually substitute a 'hands team' for their normal return unit when they know an opponent is likely to kick the onside.

Kick-off return

There are three groups of players positioned on the kick-off return. The first line consists of five **blockers**, linemen or linebackers, who line up ten yards away from the ball (to prevent the sneak or onside kick) on the opponents' 45-yard line. Once the ball is kicked they retreat around 15 yards to set up blocks for the returners.

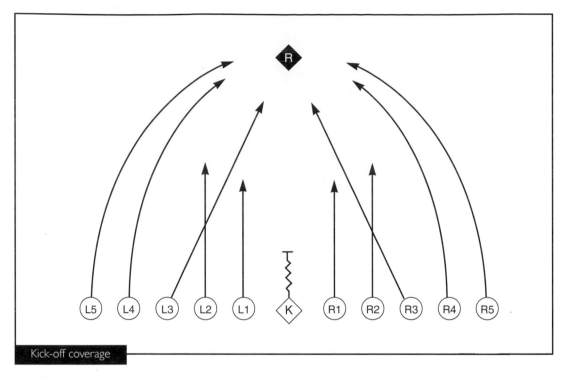

The second group comprises a three- or four-man **wedge** of blockers, who position themselves around the 25-yard line. The wedge men have the task of clearing a path for the returners behind them by blocking the first wave of tacklers.

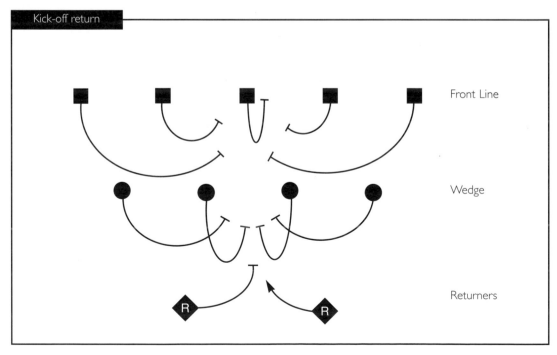

Front Line

Wedge

Returners

The third group, positioned near the goal line, consist of two or three **returners** whose job it is to receive the kick and head back up field at speed to gain as much yardage as possible. One of the most spectacular and momentum-shifting plays in gridiron is when a returner uses his blockers and takes the kick-off all the way back to the opponents' endzone for a touchdown.

The field goal

There are two ways a team can score by kicking the ball: with the field goal or point after touchdown conversion. In both cases the ball must be kicked from a spot on the ground, positioned by a holder, between the uprights and over the crossbar of the goalposts. In the World League field goals are worth three points and four if measuring 50 or more yards.

The extra point or point after touchdown (PAT) kick is worth one point and is kicked only after a touchdown has been scored. The ball is placed at the two-yard line where it is snapped by the centre back to the holder (usually around seven yards away) for the kicker to kick. With the goalposts sitting ten yards back from the goal line a PAT, depending on where it is spotted, usually measures 19 yards in length.

Punting strategy

There are three aspects to the punt game which must be considered. First, the **punt** itself, second, the **punt coverage** and third, the **punt return**.

From a **long snap** from the centre the punter will send a high kick, usually on fourth down, as close to the oppenents' goal line as possible. The punter is keen to kick the ball away from any dangerous returner but is as eager to keep the ball **in bounds** and out of the endzone to gain maximum field position. A punt which goes into or through the back of the endzone is ruled a **touch-back** and is placed at the 20-yard line, where the opponent begins their next offensive series. The punter also likes his kick to **arc** high with a **hang time** of around 4.2 or 4.4 seconds (a little longer than on the kick-off), to allow his cover men to get underneath the ball in an attempt to stop the returner immediately.

A **punt returner**, usually a speedy, sure-handed receiver, can elect to return the kick behind his return team or, if under pressure, may call for a **fair catch**, where he has to wave a signal to the official before catching the punt on the full. The fair catch **cannot be advanced** for any yardage gain: however, the cover team is not allowed to hit or tackle the returner once he has made the fair catch. If a punter catches the ball in the endzone he may elect to stoop down on one knee to stop play and bring up a touch-back.

Unlike the kick-off, an opponent must first touch the ball before it can be recovered by the punt team. As with the field goal or PAT, the coach may elect to run a **fake punt** on fourth down from the punt formation. If successful, it retains possession, gaining a first down for the offence.

Tips for Watching the Game

- Watch the quarterback. As a start, rather than searching for the ball, focus on the quarterback and watch his movements. If he drops straight back, odds on it's going to be a pass. But if he rolls or fakes, the play may be developing into a run. Having got used to the fact that the quarterback – the man with all the options – will be floating around the backfield, you will start to see the wider picture.

- Be aware of the game situation and try to predict the next play. Knowing the offensive down, the distance it has to go and what part of the field they are on will give you a vital clue as to what the play will be. E.g. On a first down play from their own five-yard line, the offence will probably call a conservative run play such as a dive to get themselves out of the danger area. On a third down with 20 yards to go a pass is a certainty.

- Look at the offensive and defensive formations, another good way to get clues on what type of play will develop. If an offence lines up with three wide receivers they are probably going to pass. If a defence stacks linebackers up at the line of scrimmage they could be getting ready to blitz.

- Watch the offensive line. Keying in on the guards is what the linebackers do to tell them if it's a run or pass. If the line stands up and drops back rapidly it may be a pass play, whereas if the offensive line stays low and shoots forward a run play has probably been called.

- On special teams, don't watch the ball. Look at the coverage men. You'll see some great hits, blocking and collisions as the players pursue downfield on kick-offs and punts. Also keep your eye on the rushers on punts, field goals and extra points. If they are getting good penetration through the line you may see a blocked kick.

- When the play stops or a team takes a time-out, the natural tendency is to look at what the cheerleaders are doing. Instead, have a look at the head coach and his assistants on the sideline and think about what play he is liable to call, given the game situation. Some interesting conversations take place on the sideline and in the huddles during these crucial periods.

- Once you know the basics, concentrate on a different part of the action. You will learn more about a position by focusing in on one player than looking at the overall action. Try looking at the lines or 'trenches', then focus on the defensive backs, linebackers or wide receivers.

- Watch out for the sneaky play. A quarterback may drop back to pass but instead hand off to a running back on the draw play. Look out for the fake punt or field goal, and towards the end of the second or fourth quarters, if the game is close, look out for the onside kick.

Glossary of Gridiron Terms

A

Audible: A change of play shouted in code at the line of scrimmage.

B

Backfield: The area behind the line of scrimmage where the running backs set and the quarterback passes. Also a term used for the running backs and quarterback.

Bench: Area on sideline where coaches, teams and substitutes gather. Pass route run towards this area.

Blindside: Tackling a player, usually the quarterback, from behind.

Blitz: A pass rush involving defensive backs individually or within a combination of backs or linebackers. Can be timed on snap or delayed.

Blocking: Deliberate and legal obstruction of an opposing player. The blocker is restricted in the following ways:
(a) he is not allowed to use his hands to grab or hold
(b) he is not allowed to use his arms to encircle or trip
(c) the block must be from a frontal direction.

Bomb: A deep pass.

Bootleg: A run by the quarterback where he fakes a handoff, hides the ball and runs the other way.

Bump and run: A pass defence technique where the pass defender bumps a receiver at the line, then trails him downfield.

C

Chain crew: The officials on the sidelines who operate the ten-yard measuring chain.

Chuck: A quick shove or push of an opponent who is in front of a defender. Used against receivers.

Clipping: An illegal block caused by throwing the body across the back of an opponent. Legal within three yards of the line of scrimmage. Usually occurs illegally downfield on punts, kick-offs and interceptions.

Completion: Successful catch of a forward pass.

Coverage: Pass defence. Also used to designate the exact type of pass defence used, e.g. 'double coverage' or 'zone coverage'.

Crackback: An illegal block thrown by any offensive player who has lined up more than two yards outside the tackle and comes towards the ball.

Usually carried out by wide receivers on linebackers.

Crossbar: Horizontal bar of a goalpost over which the field goal or extra point must be kicked to score.

Cross block: When two offensive linemen exchange assignments, each taking the other's man.

Cut: A sidestep or reverse of direction when running at speed, also called cutback. Can also refer to practice of dropping or releasing players from the team when trimming roster sizes down.

D

Dead ball: When the ball can no longer be advanced and is whistled dead by the officials. Penalties committed after the whistle are called 'dead ball fouls'.

Defence: The team without possession of the ball. The tactics of that team.

Defensive backs: Men who play in defensive secondary – cornerback and safeties.

Delay of game: The quarterback fails to initiate play before 35-second game clock winds down. Five-yard penalty.

Deuce: Two-point score unique to World League where defence returns blocked extra point attempt into opponents' endzone.

Dime: A pass defence featuring six defensive backs.

Dog: Pass rush involving linebackers individually or in combination.

Double coverage: Two defensive players converging on one receiver.

Double teaming: Two offensive blockers working on one defender.

Down: A play from the line of scrimmage. The offence gets four to move the ball, gain a first down and retain possession.

Draft: The annual World League and NFL player selection meetings.

Draw: A delayed fake pass run play.

Drop: The movement of the quarterback after the snap as he retreats into the backfield to set up to pass. Also relates to the movement of the linebackers and defensive backs as they retreat into pass coverage.

E

Ejection: When a player is sent off by the referee for a serious infraction of the rules. In the World League a player may be ejected for two plays for an unnecessary roughness penalty.

Encroachment: Penalty called if player is in neutral zone as ball is snapped or makes contact with opponent before ball is snapped.

End around: A variation of the reverse play in which the tight end or wide receiver becomes the ball carrier on a sweep.

Endzone: Area ten yards deep bounded by goal line, endline and both sidelines where touchdowns/safeties/deuces are scored.

Extra point: One-point coversion scored after touchdown by kicking ball through goalposts. Also called PAT or point after touchdown.

F

Fair catch: An unhindered catch called by the receiver of a punt or kick-off. To signal a fair catch the player must raise one arm above his head. Once he makes fair catch he cannot run or be tackled.

Fake: Deception by quarterback or running back in handling the ball. Deception by coach in aligning one way and running different play, as in fake punt.

False start: Penalty called when interior offensive lineman moves after assuming three-point stance. Quarterback may also be called for false start by 'bobbing' his head in attempt to draw defence offside.

Field: Area measuring 120 yards by 53⅓ feet marked with lines within which game is played.

Field goal: Scoring kick worth three points, four if kicked 50 or more yards in World League.

Flag: Yellow cloth thrown by officials to indicate penalty on play.

Flanker: Wide receiver on tight end's side of field.

Flare pass: Short pass to running back, usually in the flat.

Flats: Backfield area near each sideline.

Flea flicker: Term originally used to describe passing play on which a receiver, immediately after catching the ball, laterals to a trailing team-mate. Also used to identify a number of other pass 'gadget' plays.

Flood: To run more receivers into an area than there are defenders to cover them.

Fly: Long pass pattern where receiver runs full speed in straight line downfield. Also called 'go' pattern.

Force: Defensive responsibility of a safety or cornerback to turn a running play towards the middle of the field and towards his team-mates.

Formation: The alignment of offensive or defensive players on a play.

Forward progress: The furthest point of a ball carrier's advancement before he is driven back by defenders. Critical factor in spotting a ball after play close to first down.

Free agent: A player who can be signed by any club.

Front: Players on defence lined up at line of scrimmage.

Fumble: Loss of possession of the football by the ball carrier, handler or passer.

G

Gadget play: A trick play.

Gameplan: The stategy and list of plays chosen by the coaches before the game.

Gap: The space between two offensive linemen. A type of run control defence that aligns a man in every gap.

Goal line: Vertical plane between the endzone and field of play that must be broken to score a touchdown.

H

Handoff: Giving the ball, hand to hand, to another player.

Hashmarks: Dotted marks running parallel in two lines down middle of field – 70 feet, nine inches from each sideline – on, or within, which the ball is spotted.

Holding: Penalty called for illegal grabbing or grasping.

Hole: Space opened by blockers for ball carrier, usually numbered on offensive line.

Huddle: Brief gathering of offence, defence or special teams players for assigments prior to start of play.

Hurry-up offence: *see* 'Two-minute offence'.

I

Incomplete pass: A pass that is not caught or intercepted.

Ineligible receiver: Offensive player not legally entitled to catch forward pass.

Ineligible receiver downfield: Penalty where ineligible receiver, usually interior lineman, has moved more than one yard downfield before ball has been thrown on pass play.

Influence: Deception by the offensive line, denying keys to the defence and leading it away from the play as in a trap or misdirection play.

Inside: Area between offensive tackles where running plays are directed.

Intentional grounding: Penalty called when quarterback purposely throws the ball away to avoid being tackled for a loss.

Interception: Change of possession when a defensive player catches a pass intended for an offensive player.

Interference: Penalty called when either an offensive or defensive player interferes with another player's efforts to catch a pass.

K

Keeper: Play where quarterback keeps ball and runs with it.

Key: Alignment or movement which helps a defensive player to tell where the ball is going or what blocks to expect.

Knuckle ball: Poorly thrown pass which, instead of rotating in line, tumbles. Also referred to as a 'wounded duck'.

L

Lateral: Pass to side or back to team-mate.

Lead block: Block by running back (usually the full-back) preceding another runner (usually half-back) through the line of scrimmage and into the first tackler.

Line call: Signals shouted at the line of scrimmage, generally by the centre, to alert the offensive linemen to their blocking assignments.

Line of scrimmage: Imaginary line dividing offence and defence which passes through the ball from sideline to sideline.

M

Man-to-man: One against one defensive coverage.

Midfield stripe: The 50-yard line.

Misdirection: Deception by the offensive backfield designed to fool defence away from true flow of play.

Motion: Predetermined movement by one offensive player, usually a receiver, parallel to the line of scrimmage before the ball is snapped.

Muff: The touching of the ball by a player in an unsuccessful attempt to gain possession of a free ball.

N

National rule: Ruling unique to World League which deems that teams must play a non-American, home-based or European player on 50 per cent of offensive and defensive plays, i.e. every alternate series or 'National series'.

Neutral zone: The space, the length of the ball, between the offence's and defence's lines.

Nickel defence: A defensive formation in which an extra (fifth) pass defender, the nickel back, is brought into the game.

No huddle offence: Offence which does not huddle between plays, relying instead on audible from quarterback. Designed to keep defence from setting up and maximise the seconds remaining on clock in situation when time is running out.

O

Offence: The team in possession of the ball. The tactics of that team.

Offside: Penalty called when a player is across the line of scrimmage at the time the ball is snapped.

Onside kick: A short kick-off that carries just beyond the required ten yards, allowing the kicking team a chance to recover the free ball.

Option pass: A play in which the quarterback has the option of throwing to any one of a number of players. Or, a play in which the runner has the option to run or pass, and passes.

Option run: A running play in which the quarterback moves down the line and has the option to handoff or pitch to a running back or run with the ball himself.

Option runner: A running back adept at rushing without predetermining a hole in the line, allowing him to run wherever he sees open space. Also called 'running to daylight'.

Outside: The area outside the offensive tackles where running plays can be directed.

Overtime: The extra ten-minute period in the World League (15 mins in the NFL) added on to the regulation 60 minutes when a game is tied. In World League rules both teams must have one possession and a chance to score before the game goes into sudden death, where the first team to score wins the game.

P

Pass block: Block executed by offensive linemen on pass play to protect the quarterback and give him time to pass the ball.

Pass interference: Illegal contact made by either offensive or defensive player in an attempt to catch or intercept a forward pass.

Pass pattern: Also called pass route. The predetermined route a receiver runs on his way to catching a pass.

Pass rush: The charge to sack or pressure the quarterback as he attempts to pass by the defence, usually the line.

Penalty: An infraction of the rules, indicated by the

officials throwing a yellow penalty marker or flag, that may result in a loss of yards, and/or down, or nullification of a play or ejection of a player.

Personal foul: Act of violent conduct outside the rules of the game, e.g. clipping or punching an opponent.

Pile: A mound of players, one on top of the other, created sometimes at the end of a play in the process of tackling.

Piling on: The term used for unnecessary and dangerous addition of players to top of the pile at end of play when ball carrier is clearly down.

Pitchout: Underhanded toss from quarterback to running back.

Play action: A play where the quarterback fakes the handoff then passes the ball.

Pocket: Protected area around a quarterback set up by pass blocking offensive linemen.

Possession: Control of the ball by an individual or team.

Post pattern: A pass route which goes downfield then breaks inside towards the goalpost.

Power sweep: A run around the end with both guards pulling to lead the blocking.

Prevent defence: Defence designed specifically to stop long passes.

Pull: When an offensive lineman (as with guard during power sweep) leaves his position to lead a play.

Punt: High kick used on fourth down to gain field position on change of possession.

Q

Quarter: 15-minute playing period; four quarters make up game.

Quarterback sneak: Short yardage play in which the quarterback takes the snap and dives over the centre.

Quick count: A short signal count designed to catch the defence off guard.

Quick hitter: A short yardage, inside running play.

R

Read: Quarterback's observation of the defensive alignment at the line. Observation of keys or action of the offence by a defensive player.

Reverse: A running play in which the quarterback hands off to a ball carrier going in the opposite direction to the flow of the play. There are a number of variations including end around and various passing options.

Rollout: Action of the quarterback as he moves across the backfield sideways to set up to pass the ball (as opposed to straight dropback). Also a play based on this action.

Rotation: When the defence shifts its zone pass coverage to the left or right.

Roughing the kicker/passer: Deliberate, forceful and illegal contact with the kicker or passer by the defender outwith one step of the kicker or passer after he has kicked the ball or thrown the pass.

Rushing play: Running with the ball following a handoff, pitchout or lateral.

Rushing yardage: The distance in yards a running back or a team has run during a game.

S

Sack: When a quarterback is tackled in possession of the ball behind the line of scrimmage for a loss of yards.

Safety: A two-point scoring play created when a defender tackles the ball carrier in the endzone, the ball is snapped or carried by an offensive player through the back of the endzone or when an offensive penalty is called in the endzone.

Scramble: When the quarterback runs to avoid being sacked.

Screen pass: A delayed passing play in which a run is faked before the ball is thrown to a running back or receiver behind a wall of blockers.

Seams: The areas between zones.

Secondary: The defensive backfield area and/or the defensive backs.

Set: The offensive or defensive alignment. Also relates to the action of an offensive player going into a three-point stance.

Shift: Movement of two or more offensive players before snap. Can also apply to movement of defence prior to snap.

Shotgun: Offensive formation in which quarterback is lined up five to seven yards behind the centre for long snap.

Sideline: Similar to touchline in rugby delimiting the out of bounds down the sides of the field.

Snap: Action of centre passing the ball between his legs to the quarterback, punter or holder to begin play. Direct snap: Snap that goes straight to runner on run play or fake. Long snap: When a ball is snapped a distance to punter or quarterback as in shotgun formation.

Snap count: The signal on which the ball is snapped.

Spearing: The illegal and dangerous act of driving at a player, helmet first, when he is on the ground.

Special teams: The offence and defensive units used on kick-offs, punts, extra points and field goals.

Spike: When a player slams the ball to the ground after scoring a touchdown.

Split: Distance between offensive linemen on the line. Formation similar to pro with the running backs aligned split behind the guards.

Spot: The placement of the ball.

Spread: An offensive formation with no running backs in the backfield. 'Run and shoot' offence is variation of spread.

Squib kick: Kick-off that is intentionally kicked low to bounce, thus being difficult to handle for the returner.

Stance: 'Ready' position adopted by players before start of play. Two-point stance, predominantly used by receivers, linebackers and defensive backs with both feet set in 'ready' position. Three-point, used by linemen, running backs which has three points of contact with ground – two feet and one hand, allowing squat position with better explosive leverage. Four point, used by linemen on all fours to 'submarine' or get under opposing block.

Strong side: The side of the offensive formation with the most receivers (usually denoted by the tight end).

Sweep: A run wide around the end.

T

Tackling: Bringing down or stopping the progress of a ball carrier by wrapping the arms around and driving to the ground.

Time-out: A halt to the game action called by either team or the referee. Each team is allowed to call three charged 90-second time-outs per half.

Touchback: When the ball is whistled dead on or behind a team's own goal line. The ball is then placed at the team's 20-yard line.

Touchdown: A six-point scoring play which occurs when the team in possession breaks the plane of the other team's goal line by running or passing the ball into it.

Trap: A running play in which the defensive lineman is influenced across the line of scrimmage, then is blocked by a pulling guard or tackle.

Two-minute offence: A time-conserving, quick play (usually passing) attack used primarily in the last two minutes of the game or the half. Also called the 'two-minute drill' or 'hurry-up offence'.

Two-minute warning: The notification given to both benches by the officials that two minutes remain in the second and fourth quarters.

U

Unnecessary roughness: Penalty called when player carries out illegal act, such as driving a quarterback into the ground after he has been stopped, that may injure an opponent.

Unsportsmanlike conduct: Penalty that covers anything from kicking or punching an opponent to swearing at an official and which is generally regarded as ungentlemanly conduct.

Up-back: A blocking back on a punt play who lines up behind his linemen. The receivers set in front of the deep receivers on kicks.

Uprights: Two vertical poles of the goalposts extending from the crossbar between which a field goal or extra point must pass.

W

Waivers: A method of allowing a player either to be claimed by another club or to become a free agent.

Weakside: The side of the offence's formation with the least number of receivers.

World League: Six-team European league made up of Amsterdam Admirals; Barcelona Dragons; Dusseldorf Rhein Fire; Frankfurt Galaxy; London Monarchs and Scottish Claymores, playing a ten-week season from April to June for the World Bowl trophy.

Y

Yardage: The distance in gridiron measured in yards.

Z

Zone: An assigned area of the field the defence covers in pass situations.

APPENDIX 3

1996 Scottish Claymores Statistics

1996 SCOTTISH CLAYMORES ALPHABETICAL ROSTER

NO.	PLAYER	POS	HEIGHT (FT/M)	WEIGHT (LBS/KG)	BIRTHDATE	COLLEGE	HOW ACQ.
56	Ale, Arnold	LB	6-2/1.88	228/103	17/6/70	UCLA	D7-96
13	Ballard, Jim	QB	6-3/1.91	225/102	16/4/72	Mount Union	NFL-95
71	Barndt, Tom	C	6-3/1.91	290/132	14/3/72	Pittsburgh	NFL/Chiefs
72	Bierman, Randy	T	6-4/1.93	320/146	30/4/71	Illinois	D27-95
70	Buck, Jason	DE	6-5/1.96	280/127	27/7/63	Brigham Young	FA-96
34	Coghill, George	S	6-0/1.83	215/98	30/3/70	Wake Forest	D13-95
81	Couper, Scott	WR	6-0/1.83	165/75	1/6/70	Strathclyde Univ	National
92	Dausin, Chris	CG	6-5/1.96	290/132	18/12/69	Texas A&M	FA-96
97	DeWitt, John	DE	6-4/1.93	270/123	30/11/70	Vanderbilt	D4-96
23	Dickerson, Ron	RB	6-1/1.85	228/103	13/8/71	Arkansas	D12-96
42	Duckett, Forey	CB/S	6-3/1.91	194/88	5/2/70	Nevado-Reno	NFL/Saints
91	Flickinger, Robert	DE	6-4/1.93	245/111	21/11/71	Georgetown College	National
20	Fuller, James	S	6-0/1.83	20894	5/8/69	Portland State	Waivers-96
1	Gissendaner, Lee	WR	5-8/1.73	167/76	25/10/71	Northwestern Univ	NFL/Vikings
15	Hastings, Gavin	K	6-2/1.88	206/93	3/1/62	Paisley/Cambridge	National
80	Hill, Derek	WR	6-2/1.88	192/87	4/11/67	Arizona	FA-96
79	Hunt, Purvis	G	6-4/1.93	383/174	25/11/70	Mississippi State	NFL/Oilers
99	Jeffcoat, Jerold	DT	6-2/1.88	280/127	30/8/69	Temple	D12-95
58	Jones, Shannon	LB	6-4/1.93	245/111	25/9/70	Southern California	D2-96
7	Jones, Khari	QB	5-11/1.80	195/89	16/5/71	UC Davis	FA-96
31	Kaaiohelo, Jared	RB	6-0/1.83	236/108	8/10/72	Missouri Southern	D22-96
88	LaChapelle, Sean	WR	6-3/1.91	205/93	29/7/70	UCLA	NFL/Chiefs
12	Matthews, Steve	QB	6-3/1.91	209/95	13/10/70	Memphis State	NFL/Chiefs
5	McCallum, Paul	K/P	5-11/1.80	190/87	7/1/70	None	National
83	Murphy, Yo	WR	5-10/1.78	187/85	11/5/71	Univ of Idaho	D3-96
86	Nummi, Jukka-Pekka	CB	6-2/1.88	180/82	16/1/71	None	Nat/Finland
90	O'Brien, Joe	DT	6-2/1.88	285/130	11/6/72	Boise State	D19-96
67	Proby, Bryan	DT	6-5/1.96	283/129	30/11/71	Arizona State	NFL/Chiefs
43	Robinson, Frank	DB	5-10/1.78	176/81	11/1/69	Boise State Univ	D6-96
54	Sander, Mark	LB	6-2/1.88	232/106	21/3/68	Louisville	D4-95
75	Spencer, James	OL	6-5/1.96	315/143	1/9/70	Syracuse	FA-95
69	Simon, Moke	DT	6-2/1.88	330/148	24/6/72	Texas	A&IFA-96
27	Stacy, Siran	RB	5-10/1.78	195/89	6/8/68	Alabama	D5-95

NO.	PLAYER	POS	HEIGHT (FT/M)	WEIGHT (LBS/KG)	BIRTHDATE	COLLEGE	HOW ACQ.
98	Storm, Matt	G/TE	6-4/1.93	321/145	2/9/72	Georgia	NFL/Redskins
85	Tate, Willy	TE	6-2/1.88	243/110	7/8/72	Oregon	NFL/Chiefs
40	Thomas, Markus	RB	5-10/1.78	200/91	12/7/70	Eastern Kentucky	D24-95
44	Torriero, Ben	RB	5-11/1.80	226/103	24/3/65	Heriots	National
78	Wagner, Keith	T	6-4/1.93	308/140	22/1/70	Abilene Christian	NFL/Redskins
51	Waldron, Emmett	LB	6-1/1.85	238/109	18/10/71	Rice	Nat/Ireland
59	Webb, David	DE	6-4/1.93	250/114	14/11/69	Southern California	D16-95
22	Williams, James	CB	5-10/1.78	185/84	8/10/70	Texas Southern	D35-95
25	Wilson, David	S	5-11/1.80	205/93	10/6/70	California	D8-95
61	Zeno, Lance	C	6-4/1.93	300/136	15/4/67	UCLA	NFL/Rams

HEAD COACH: Jim Criner
ASSISTANT COACHES: Ray Willsey, Jim Sochor, Bill Dutton, Larry Owens, Vince Alcalde, Mike Kenny
Football Support Staff: Darin Kerns, Mark Riederer, Bill Robinette, Brian Farr, Wayne 'Smitty' Smith, John Osnowitz

SCOTTISH CLAYMORES STATISTICS

PASSING	ATT	CMP	YDS	CMP%	YDS/ATT	TD	TD%	INT	INT%	LONG	SACK/LOST	RATING
Ballard, J.	67	50	787	74.6	11.75	8	11.9	2	2.9	76	7/53	143.5
Jones, K.	1	1	9	100.0	9.00	0	0.0	0	0.0	9	0/0	104.2
Matthews, S.	205	115	1560	56.1	7.61	9	4.3	10	4.8	52t	16/93	74.9
Karg, T.	1	0	0	0.0	0.00	0	0.0	0	0.0	0	0/0	39.6
Scottish Total	274	166	2356	60.6	8.60	17	6.2	12	4.4	76	23/14	90.9
Opponents Total	391	219	2413	56.0	6.16	16	4.1	19	4.9	57t	25/15	67.9

SACKS

Jeffcoat, J. 5.0, Carroll, H. 3.5, O'Brien, J. 2.5, Parten, T. 2.5, Sander, M. 2.0, Coghill, G. 1.5, Fuller, J. 1.0, Ridgley, T. 1.0, Webb, D. 1.0, Williams, J. 1.0, Jones, S. 0.5

Scottish Total   25.0
Opponents Total 23.0

DEFENSE

	TT	UT	AT	SACK	PD	FF	SPEC TACK	MISC TACK	BLOCKED KICKS P	FG	PAT
Coghill, G.	61	58	3	1.5	9	1	3	0	0	0	0
Sander, M.	51	49	2	2.0	2	2	2	0	0	0	0
Fuller, J.	43	39	4	1.0	9	0	4	0	0	0	0
Jones, S.	36	29	7	0.5	2	1	2	0	0	0	0
Williams, J.	35	31	4	1.0	11	0	3	0	0	0	0
Duckett, F.	30	28	2	0.0	7	1	2	0	0	0	0
Ale, A.	27	27	0	0.0	2	1	0	0	0	0	0
Waldron, E.	26	25	1	0.0	0	1	3	0	0	0	0
Wilson, D.	19	17	2	0.0	2	0	3	0	0	0	0
Jeffcoat, J.	15	15	0	5.0	0	0	0	0	0	0	0
Parten, T.	13	13	0	2.5	2	0	0	0	0	0	0
Carroll, H.	12	11	1	3.5	2	0	2	0	0	0	0
Robinson, F.	11	11	0	0.0	4	1	5	0	0	0	0
Ridgley, T.	10	10	0	1.0	0	0	0	0	0	0	0
DeWitt, J.	9	8	1	3.5	0	1	3	0	0	0	0
Webb, D.	9	8	1	1.0	0	0	2	0	0	0	0
Proby, B.	8	7	1	0.0	0	0	0	0	0	0	0
O'Brien, J.	6	6	0	2.5	0	0	2	0	0	0	0
McGill, K.	2	1	1	0.0	0	0	3	0	0	0	0
Goodwin, M.	1	1	0	0.0	1	0	1	0	0	0	0
Zeno, L.	0	0	0	0.0	0	0	0	1	0	0	0
Dickerson, R.	0	0	0	0.0	0	0	0	1	0	0	0
Gissendaner, L.	0	0	0	0.0	0	0	0	1	0	0	0
Hastings, G.	0	0	0	0.0	0	0	1	0	0	0	0
Kaaiohelo, J.	0	0	0	0.0	0	0	2	2	0	0	0
LaChappelle, S.	0	0	0	0.0	0	0	0	1	0	0	0
McCallum, P.	0	0	0	0.0	0	0	3	0	0	0	0
Murphy, Y.	0	0	0	0.0	0	0	0	2	0	0	0
Storm, M.	0	0	0	0.0	0	0	2	0	0	0	0
Tate, W.	0	0	0	0.0	0	0	0	1	0	0	0
Flickinger, R.	0	0	0	0.0	1	0	2	0	0	0	0
Stacy, S.	0	0	0	0.0	0	0	0	2	0	0	0
Thomas, M.	0	0	0	0.0	0	0	4	0	0	0	0
Torriero, B.	0	0	0	0.0	0	0	3	0	0	0	0

WORLD BOWL 96 DEPTH CHART
SCOTTISH CLAYMORES v. FRANKFURT GALAXY
MURRAYFIELD STADIUM – 23 JUNE 1996

OFFENCE

SE	#83 YO MURPHY	#80 DEREK HILL	#86 JUKKA-PEKKA NUMMI
LT	#72 RANDY BIERMAN	#75 JAMES SPENCER	
LG	#71 TOM BARNDT	#98 MATT STORM	
C	#61 LANCE ZENO	#92 CHRIS DAUSIN	
RG	#79 PURVIS HUNT	#98 MATT STORM	
RT	#78 KEITH WAGNER	#72 RANDY BIERMAN	
TE	#85 WILLY TATE	#98 MATT STORM	#91 ROBERT FLICKINGER
FL	#88 SEAN LaCHAPELLE	#81 SCOTT COUPER	
QB	#13 JIM BALLARD	#12 STEVE MATTHEWS	#7 KHARI JONES
FB	#23 RON DICKERSON	#31 JARED KAAIHELO	#44 BEN TORRIERO
TB	#27 SIRAN STACY	#40 MARKUS THOMAS	

NATIONAL STARTER   #81 SCOTT COUPER (FL)

DEFENCE

LE	#90 JOE O'BRIEN	#59 DAVID WEBB	
LT	#67 BRYAN PROBY	#69 MOKE SIMON	
RT	#99 JEROLD JEFFCOAT	#69 MOKE SIMON	
RE	#97 JOHN DEWITT	#92 JASON BUCK	#91 ROBERT FLICKENGER
SAM	#58 SHANNON JONES		
MLB	#54 MARK SANDER	#51 EMMETT WALDRON	
WIL	#56 ARNOLD ALE		
LCB	#42 FOREY DUCKETT	#43 FRANK ROBINSON	
RCB	#22 JAMES WILLIAMS	#43 FRANK ROBINSON	
SS	#34 GEORGE COGHILL	#25 DAVID WILSON	
FS	#20 JAMES FULLER	#25 DAVID WILSON	

NATIONAL STARTER   #51 EMMETT WALDRON (MLB)

SPECIALISTS

LS	#90 JOE O'BRIEN	#85 WILLY TATE
H	#13 JIM BALLARD	#85 WILLY TATE
KO	#15 GAVIN HASTINGS	
PAT	#15 GAVIN HASTINGS	
FG	#5 PAUL McCALLUM	
P	#5 PAUL McCALLUM	#44 BEN TORRIERO
KOR	#40 MARKUS THOMAS	#23 RON DICKERSON
PR	#40 MARKUS THOMAS	

1996 WORLD LEAGUE LEADERS

TOUCHDOWNS

	TD	RUS	REC	RET	PTS
S. Stacy, Sco	9	7	2	0	54
B. Chamberlain, Rhe	8	0	8	0	48
S. LaChappelle, Sco	7	0	7	0	42
A. Browning, Bar	6	0	6	0	36
J. Kearney, Fran	6	0	6	0	36
Y. Murphy, Sco	5	0	5	0	30
T. Vinson, Lon	5	3	2	0	30
T.C. Wright, Ams	5	2	2	1	30
P. Bobo, Ams	4	0	4	0	24
B. Phillips, Fran	4	4	0	0	24
T. Wilburn, Bar	4	3	1	0	24
I. Seibert, Fran	4	4	0	0	24
D. Jones, Ams	4	0	4	0	24

KICKING

	PAT	FG	LG	PTS
S. Szeredy, Bar	15/17	9/13	47	42
R. Kleinmann, Fran	23/25	6/13	42	41
P. McCallum, Sco	0/0	11/15	51	34
A. Vinatieri, Ams	4/4	9/10	43	31
H. Werdekker, Ams	27/28	0/0	0	27
L. Araguz, Rhe	0/0	8/15	40	24
R. Ruzek, Lon	0/0	8/11	39	24
G. Hastings, Sco	23/27	0/1	0	23
M. Burgsmuller, Rhe	17/19	1/3	22	20
K. Hurst, Lon	17/19	0/0	0	17

LEADING PASSERS

	ATT	COMP	PCT COMP	YDS	AVG GAIN	TD	PCT TD	LONG	INT	PCT INT	RATING POINTS
W. Furrer, Ams	368	206	56.0	2689	7.31	20	5.4	48	13	3.5	82.6
S. Pelluer, Fran	283	165	58.3	2136	7.55	11	3.9	90t	12	4.2	77.4
K. Holcomb, Bar	319	191	59.9	2382	7.47	14	4.4	87t	16	5.0	76.9
A. Kelly, Rhe	245	149	60.8	1333	5.44	9	3.7	44t	7	2.9	75.8
S. Matthews, Sco	205	115	56.1	1560	7.61	9	4.4	52t	10	4.9	74.9
P. Jones, Lon	295	152	51.5	1649	5.59	12	4.1	59	7	2.4	72.0

RECEPTIONS

	NO	YDS	AVG	LONG	TD
B. Chamberlain, Rhe	58	685	11.8	32t	8
P. Bobo, Ams	50	817	16.3	42t	4
J. Kearney, Fran	50	686	13.7	46t	6
S. LaChapelle, Sco	47	1023	21.8	76	7
B. Burnett, Bar	43	383	8.9	43	1
D. Davis, Bar	43	376	8.7	37	2
D. Smith, Ams	37	443	12.0	23	2
D. Clark, Rhe	37	229	6.2	26	0
S. Stacy, Sco	36	317	8.8	43	2
M. Bailey, Fran	35	643	18.4	69	2
G. Harrell, Fran	31	545	17.6	90t	3
D. Jones, Ams	29	464	16.0	35	4
M. Titley, Lon	29	304	10.5	32	2

continued

RECEPTIONS, continued

	NO	YDS	AVG	LONG	TD
J. Davison, Rhe	28	172	6.1	16	0
A. Browning, Bar	27	538	19.9	60t	6
W. Hinchcliff, Lon	27	363	13.4	49	2
D. Chandler, Ams	27	327	12.1	42t	3
N. Bolton, Fran	26	216	8.3	22	0
E. Howard, Lon	25	364	14.6	59	0
T. Vinson, Lon	25	169	6.8	51t	2

RECEIVING YARDS

	YDS	NO	AVG	LONG	TD
S. LaChapelle, Sco	1023	47	21.8	76	7
P. Bobo, Ams	817	50	16.3	42t	4
J. Kearney, Fran	686	50	13.7	46t	6
B. Chamberlain, Rhe	685	58	11.8	32t	8
M. Bailey, Fran	643	35	18.4	69	2
G. Harrell, Fran	545	31	17.6	90t	3
A. Browning, Bar	538	27	19.9	60t	6
D. Jones, Ams	464	29	16.0	35	4
D. Smith, Ams	443	37	12.0	23	2
B. Burnett, Bar	383	43	8.9	43	1
D. Davis, Bar	376	43	8.7	37	2
E. Howard, Lon	364	25	14.6	59	0
W. Hinchcliff, Lon	363	27	13.4	49	2
K. Shedd, Bar	328	14	23.4	57t	1
D. Chandler, Ams	327	27	12.1	42t	3
S. Stacy, Sco	317	36	8.8	43	2
M. Bellamy, Fran	313	22	14.2	41	0
L. Wallace, Lon	310	23	13.5	44	3
M. Titley, Lon	304	29	10.5	32	2
Y. Murphy, Sco	298	21	14.2	43	5

LEADING RUSHERS

	ATT	YARDS	AVG	LONG	TD
S. Stacy, Sco	208	780	3.8	43t	7
T. Vinson, Lon	105	516	4.9	67	3
C. Thompson, Bar	117	410	3.5	26	1
D. Clark, Rhe	84	399	4.8	23	3
T.C. Wright, Ams	80	379	4.7	22	2
T. Wilburn, Bar	72	249	3.5	17	3
J. Davison, Rhe	55	224	4.1	12	0
R. White, Lon	51	221	4.3	31	1
W. Furrer, Ams	26	189	7.3	46t	1
T. Cobb, Ams	53	170	3.2	32	1
G. Green, Lon	53	170	3.2	32	0
I. Seibert, Fran	72	164	2.3	12	4
T. Richardson, Rhe	36	153	4.3	20t	1
B. Phillips, Fran	49	149	3.0	20	4
N. Bolton, Fran	42	118	2.8	14	3
B. Bryant, Ams	31	113	3.6	18	0
K. Holcomb, Bar	38	111	2.9	21	2
O. Carter, Rhe	22	110	5.0	35	0
S. Matthews, Sco	26	105	4.0	34	1

TOTAL YARDS FROM SCRIMMAGE

	TOTAL	RUSH	REC
S. Stacy, Sco	1097	780	317
S. LaChapelle, Sco	1023	0	1023

TOTAL YARDS FROM SCRIMMAGE, continued

	TOTAL	RUSH	REC
P. Bobo, Ams	817	0	817
B. Chamberlain, Rhe	689	4	685
J. Kearney, Fran	686	0	686
T. Vinson, Lon	685	516	169
M. Bailey, Fran	654	11	643
D. Clark, Rhe	628	399	229
T.C. Wright, Ams	628	379	249
C. Thompson, Bar	550	410	140
G. Harrell, Fran	545	0	545
A. Browning, Bar	538	0	538
T. Wilburn, Bar	502	249	253
D. Jones, Ams	464	0	464
D. Smith, Ams	450	7	443
R. White, Lon	440	221	219
J. Davison, Rhe	396	224	172
B. Burnett, Bar	383	0	383

LEADING PUNTERS

	NO	YDS	LG	AVG	TB	BLK	RET	RET YDS	IN 20	NET AVG
S. Feexico, Lon	59	2567	62	43.5	7	1	33	555	13	31.2
L. Araguz, Rhe	41	1735	58	42.3	4	0	18	103	17	37.9
S. Edge, Bar	41	1646	52	40.1	5	0	21	185	11	33.2
A. Vinatieri, Ams	41	1612	56	39.3	4	0	17	110	12	34.7
K. Feighery, Fran	41	1520	67	37.1	4	1	16	182	13	30.0
P. McCallum, Sco	49	1720	48	35.1	2	0	20	124	9	31.8

PUNT RETURN LEADERS

	NO	YARDS	AVG	LONG	TD
T.C. Wright, Ams	17	272	16.0	85t	1
M. Marshall, Bar	20	243	12.2	47	0
T. Boyd, Rhe	17	164	9.6	20	0
K. McEntyre, Lon	19	85	4.5	14	0

INTERCEPTIONS

	INT	YARDS	LONG	TD
K. McEntyre, Lon	5	128	66t	1
D. Studstill, Lon	5	80	22	1
G. Coghill, Sco	5	73	32t	1
J. Fuller, Sco	5	46	26	0
J. Ellis, Rhe	4	90	57t	1
S. Crocker, Lon	4	76	30	0
C. Doggette, Fran	4	59	33	0
J. Dixon, Fran	4	58	43t	1
C. Hall, Fran	4	54	27t	1
J. Phillips, Ams	4	31	16	0
M. Gay, Rhe	3	97	76t	1
D. Wilson, Sco	3	39	23	0
M. Salmon, Rhe	3	18	18	0
F. Duckett, Sco	3	9	9	0

KICK-OFF RETURN LEADERS

	NO	YARDS	AVG	LONG	TD
B. Bryant, Ams	19	457	24.1	54	0
P. Grier, Lon	31	697	22.5	89t	1
M. Thomas, Sco	20	446	22.3	49	0
M. Marshall, Bar	19	419	22.1	48	0
L. Kennedy, Rhe	17	352	20.7	35	0

continued

KICK-OFF RETURN LEADERS, continued

	NO	YARDS	AVG	LONG	TD
G. Harrell, Fran	25	447	17.9	40	0
C. Thompson, Bar	18	315	17.5	33	0
T. Richardson, Rhe	15	233	15.5	24	0

SACKS

J. Drake, Lon	8.0
D. Anderson, Rhe	7.5
J. Heinrich, Bar	6.0
J. Baker, Fran	6.0
H. Morris, Lon	6.0
B. Berger, Lon	5.0
B. Hamilton, Ams	5.0
J. Jeffcoat, Sco	5.0
D. Krein, Bar	4.5
D. Reynolds, Fran	4.5
M. Byers, Fran	4.0
J. Hunter, Lon	4.0
J. Wilson, Rhe	4.0

TEAM RANKINGS

	OFFENCE			DEFENCE		
	TOTAL	RUSH	PASS	TOTAL	RUSH	PASS
Amsterdam	1	2	1	6	3	6
Barcelona	4	5	3	3	2	3
Frankfurt	3	6	2	5	6	2
London	5	4	5	1	5	1
Rhein	6	3	6	2	1	4
Scottish	2	1	4	4	4	5

TAKE AWAYS/GIVE AWAYS

	TAKE AWAYS			GIVE AWAYS				NET
	INT	FUM	TOTAL	INT	FUM	TOTAL	=	DIFF
London	16	11	27	9	8	17	=	10
Amsterdam	14	14	28	13	12	25	=	3
Frankfurt	17	12	29	19	8	27	=	2
Scottish	19	6	25	12	12	24	=	1
Rhein	11	8	19	12	9	21	=	-2
Barcelona	5	9	14	17	11	28	=	-14

TOTAL OFFENCE

	TOTAL	RUSHING	PASSING
Amsterdam	3483	970	2513
Scottish	3300	1090	2210
Frankfurt	3131	652	2479
Barcelona	3032	779	2253
London	2717	937	1780
Rhein	2708	954	1754

TOTAL DEFENCE

	TOTAL	RUSHING	PASSING
London	2843	1030	1813
Rhein	2958	720	2238
Barcelona	2999	814	2185
Scottish	3132	876	2256
Frankfurt	3178	1098	2080
Amsterdam	3261	844	2417